Good Girls
Go to
Heaven

.

Bad Girls
Go
Everywhere

How to Break
the Rules and Get
What You Want
from Your Job,
Your Family, and
Your Relationship

BY JANA U. EHRHARDT

Good Girls Go to Heaven

·

Bad Girls Go Everywhere

How to Break the Rules and Get What You Want from Your Job, Your Family, and Your Relationship

ST. MARTIN'S PRESS ✖ NEW YORK

Design by Pei Koay

Library of Congress Cataloging-in-Publication Data

Ehrhardt, Jana U.
    Good girls go to heaven, bad girls go everywhere :
    how to break the rules and get what you want from your
    job, your family, and your relationship / by Jana
    Ehrhardt; translated by Margot Dembo.—1st. ed.
        p.   cm.
    Translated from German.
    ISBN 0-312-15136-5
    1. Assertiveness in women.   2. Women—Psychology.
    3. Women in business.   4. Man-woman relationships.
    5. Family.   I. Title.
    HQ1206.E4   1997   96-41584
                                                                CIP

First published in Germany as *Gute Mädchen Kommen in
den Himmel, böse überall hin: Warum Bravsein uns nicht
weiterbringt* by Wolfgang Krüger Verlag

First U.S. Edition: March 1997

10   9   8   7   6   5   4   3   2   1

I know no sure road to success,

only the road to certain failure:

trying to please everybody

PLATO

Contents

Chapter 1

Contents

Contents

Chapter 5

Chapter 6

Chapter 7

Contents

Chapter 8

Chapter 9

———

Chapter 10

———

Contents

Chapter 11

**Bad Girls Get to Go Everywhere—Even to Heaven . . .
on Earth!**

Good Girls
Go to
Heaven

.

Bad Girls
Go
Everywhere

How to Break
the Rules and Get
What You Want
from Your Job,
Your Family, and
Your Relationship

Being Good,
from the Cradle
to the Grave

·

Women are the good sex. We are expected to be friendly, compliant, modest, and generous. At a young age, we learned that being good is the key to success, when, in fact, the opposite is true.

Today women are starting to look at themselves a little differently and they are no longer satisfied with merely being good. But this New Woman is still struggling with a lot of contradictory feelings. She may assert herself, but not without a twinge of guilt. On the outside, she may appear calm, but on the inside, she is continually grappling with self-doubt. On the one hand, the New Woman still wants to be liked by everybody and tries to please everyone. On the other hand, she knows this will only lead to entangling relationships and her dependence on others. She wants to take charge, but without stepping on other people's toes; she wants to realize her goals, but she doesn't want to use cutthroat tactics; she wants to be critical, but she doesn't want to hurt anyone's feelings; she wants to speak her mind and convince others she is right, but she doesn't want to be manipulative; she wants to express her ideas, but not to the point where she intimidates other people.

Her hidden self-doubts rise to the surface through the subtle nuances in her body language: a slightly inclined head, a barely perceptible questioning look, a shy smile—all these signals alert others to her lack of confidence. A seemingly insignificant gesture can actually send out self-defeating messages such as "Go ahead and change my mind" or "My resistance is only halfhearted."

Women find it easy to empathize. They understand how and why someone else feels a certain way, which is why it's difficult for them to impose their own wishes on others or stick up for their own opinions.

When we look at the model "wife" in some TV programs today, we often find a perfect but compliant woman who does it all. With a smile, she copes with a household, her career, children, and her duties as wife. She makes sacrifices to support her husband's career. Remember Mary Tyler Moore on "The Dick Van Dyke Show," Phylicia Rashad on "The Cosby Show," and Patricia Richardson on Tim Allen's "Home Improvement"? Aside from being beautiful, physically fit, well groomed, and tireless, she is also considerate, yielding, and always ready to help others without any expectation of thanks or gratitude. She is forever the smiling partner whose role is to support and remain in the background.

Anxiety and depression plague women more frequently than men, and one cannot help but surmise that this phenomenon has something to do with the fact that women have to accomplish more than men in order to achieve equal recognition or status. In the workplace, women often work harder than their male colleagues, and yet they are not paid as well as men are and are not promoted commensurately. Any success she may experience from her job is usually on a lower level of the office power structure. Women try hard to be better, to work harder, to be prepared to compromise, to be more helpful and more cooperative than their male colleagues, but their constructive efforts are rewarded only modestly.

The old proverb lingers: There's no reward without effort—no gain without pain. And so women wear themselves out, but unfortunately, their efforts are often futile. Women build up the groundwork and help others, naively believing that this docile attitude will push them up the ladder. They back up their male colleagues or husbands who feast on the fruits of female labor. Have you ever noticed that most assistants and secretaries are female? Only women who have learned to employ clever strategies get to the top—these women have learned that working for others will not lead to success. Modesty is not the best means to achieve goals, and yet many women conceal their accomplishments because they don't want to boast or show off. Instead, they wait to be discovered, and if nobody recognizes their talents, they become frustrated and prickly, and eventually, even depressed or burned-out.

According to one company executive, "women are born to serve" and should work only in the services sector, where they can become independent on a small scale. "Service," he insisted, "is part of their nature." Unfortunately, many women prove him right: They do exactly what is expected of them; they don't dare break out of the stereotype; they don't try to advertise their good ideas. By being nice and tolerant, they think they will succeed in their careers and in their private lives. They hope to keep a man by being understanding and yielding, by relieving him of inconvenient tasks. In return for their helpfulness and drudgery, they hope to earn praise and affection. They still believe in the example of their mothers, even though experience has long ago taught them that it's the audacious woman, the fresh and rebellious one, who gets ahead—never the "good" one.

Women often make unrealistically high demands of themselves and don't value success if it comes too easily. They exert themselves strenuously and achieve a great deal. But as soon as they reach their goal, something dire happens—they start to doubt themselves and feel that their success was not due to their hard work. They don't believe that their abilities could possibly bring on positive results. If they succeed at something, they credit external circumstances, luck, or coincidence. And if they don't achieve their goal, their latent self-evaluation is confirmed: "I'm just not good enough. Somebody else would have done it better." Angry at themselves, they pull back and shy away from further challenges.

Adaptation—A Strategy with Serious Consequences

Preferring to conform to the point of becoming invisible, women don't want to stand out in a crowd. Laboring under the motto "Make yourself inconspicuous," they try hard to be unobtrusive "good" girls, fully believing that such camouflage will help them achieve their goals.

Women must learn not merely to yearn silently for gratitude but to demand a quid pro quo for services rendered. They make sacrifices believing that, in return, others will owe them something, which will some day be paid back. But normally this doesn't happen. Women must understand that *either* they do someone a favor, give him a gift—without expecting the favor to be returned—*or* they do something because they expect gratitude, recognition, or a favor in return. But this must be clearly expressed in advance. That way the other person will have the opportunity and the right to decline the favor, and then both parties will know where they stand.

The greatest stumbling block for women to overcome is that they desperately want to be liked. And for that they renounce self-determination, independence, and power. Instead of "finding" themselves, they move further and further away from themselves. If someone demonstrates high regard for them, they often will not believe it. They don't really expect to be respected, and this won't change as long as women value the opinions of others more than their own wishes and ideas.

If you want to get out of this rut, then start now. List three reasons for liking yourself. But include only reasons that can be useful to you!

Women who are in harmony with themselves have learned to balance their own needs against the demands of the world around them. They are willing to try things out and are ready to take risks. Risk taking can mean winning or losing, but these women are determined to win. Focusing on the path they have chosen, they don't obsess or worry about what others think of them. What they have discovered is that they believe in their own abilities, their know-how, and their competence. That won't make them mean or inconsiderate, but rather, courageous, more independent; they'll also have more fun.

Women who have decided to take risks do not fear setbacks. Take any sport or game as a comparison to your situation: A basketball team cannot expect to win every single point, but that does not mean they can't win in the end. Don't let a rejection take the wind out of your sails, don't take a "no" personally, and *don't,* above all, blame yourself if a situation doesn't take off as planned. If something doesn't work out, look for reasons in the matter at hand, as opposed to wasting your valuable energy on analyzing your own shortcomings. Instead of racking your brains to figure out what's wrong with you, try thinking of creative solutions instead.

Unfortunately, few women manage to take this step toward independence. Most women are stuck in old behavior patterns, opting to be good girls who take the leftovers, instead of bad girls who go for the gold. Why do women forbid themselves to take the best? Why is it so hard for women to believe that they deserve to be paid well, treated well, and listened to? Why is it women have such difficulty being bad when men do it so easily and frequently?

We are haunted by our fear of being punished for merely showing confidence, for merely bending the rules. What will others think of us? How will they behave toward us? Will they still like a "bad" girl?

Reined in by their goodness, women deny themselves a lot of the "fun things" in life. They rarely get what they really want. The causes for this self-denial go far back. Even the way a child is nursed influences his or her later behavior. Though it's hard to reconstruct the process by which children turn into girls and boys, it is only in this context that it becomes clear how female helplessness and overadaptation come into being and what it is that makes these qualities adhere so tenaciously to women.

Two psychological models were developed and refined within the last fifteen years that explain how self-limiting behavior originates and how it is perpetuated. These models show how women get bogged down in dead-end situations and why it is so hard for them to overcome self-destructive patterns of behavior.

Learned helplessness (LH) is the central concept in understanding the conflicts women face in their lives. Many everyday problems can be described as helplessness. Women behave as though they are helpless when they get a flat tire and think they can't change it. On a more extreme level, this paradigm also includes women who don't dare leave abusive husbands who beat them. Martin Seligman, one of the originators of the concept of LH, claims that dramatic psychological ills—conditions like depressions or states of anxiety—can be explained as helplessness reactions. Many different experiences can lead us to conclude: "I can't help myself." This is where anxiety and depression start. Individuals react with helplessness only because they *believe* they are not able to cope with a situation. In such a case, objective reality is not the decisive factor, but rather our own assessment based on the conviction that we ourselves have no influence on the positive outcome of a situation. The consequence is that such individuals are paralyzed into inaction.

Helplessness is learned; it is never unavoidable.

The concept of the *self-fulfilling prophesy* (SFP)* says the following: An event occurs because a corresponding expectation existed. Here is an example of the SFP attitude: "If I have certain expectations about a future event, it is more likely that I'll prepare myself to meet the actual situation when it arrives along the lines of my expectation" or "If I am afraid of an upcoming exam, I am nervous and study for it haphazardly. I imagine myself getting the wrong answers or drawing a complete blank. The probability of failing increases. The result is, my exam jitters get even worse."

---

*Robert K. Merton introduced this concept to modern sociology. The idea is mentioned even earlier (1885) by Ebbinghaus. Merton, Robert K., *The Self-Fulfilling Prophecy,* as cited by Peter H. Ludwig.

Here is a contrasting attitude that maintains an expectation of success: "If I believe I can pass the exam, I study purposefully, I am focused, and all my senses are receptive. I put my whole mind to it. I feel relaxed and sure of myself. I have a mental image of getting the right answers." The probability of passing increases. The result is the expectation of a successful outcome.

The LH and SFP patterns interlock and complement each other. The woman who believes she does not have any talent for technical things may have already absorbed that sort of defeatist message as a child. She tells herself, for example, that she can't change the spark plugs in her car. Still, she may start to do it halfheartedly, with the wrong tools and too little know-how. One of her fingers gets caught trying to get at a hard-to-reach bolt, she doesn't remember which cables go where, she breaks something, and this promptly confirms the subliminal expectation of her own helplessness. Although she believes that she really tried, she didn't solve the problem. So she generalizes this predetermined failure, and her doubts of being able to ever master mechanical or technical things increase. Deep down inside her, the matter is finally settled. What counts for her from now on is this: She needs help. Her self-created incompetence has become a fact.

Now take a woman who is not helpless and has different expectations of herself. When she changes the spark plugs, she may also get her finger caught. But she is convinced that it's no big deal, just momentary clumsiness. She looks for the cause: Her fingers were slippery, and she was using the wrong tools. She'll be more careful the next time. This little mishap won't make her doubt her competence.

Helplessness affects various everyday situations. Helpless women doubt their ability to act effectively. They rarely fulfill the goals they have hesitantly set themselves. They fall far short of their potential. They give up in the face of minor difficulties. This lack of perseverance does not necessarily apply to all areas of life. For instance, a grocer's wife who successfully deals with her husband's customers may not be able to assert herself at all in an argument with her mother. A teacher who finds it a breeze to cope with un-ruly students panics when she has to drive to an advanced teach-ers' training course. People can be competent and strong in one area and awkward and fearful in another.

Unbelievable as it may sound, positive experiences of success and accomplishment cannot be automatically carried over from one sphere to another—because the obstacles to giving yourself the credit for an accomplishment are too high. You tend to see it as merely a coincidence or a fluke. Such obstructive beliefs arise from early learning experiences. They function like roadblocks to pos-sible change. People are not held back by real obstacles, but rather by their own inner explanatory models. Anyone who believes she cannot solve a math problem because mathematical ability doesn't run in the family has set up a solid mental block. On the other hand, there's the woman who recognizes that the solution of a complex mathematical problem will be difficult and require great effort and thought, *but* she knows it can be done.

Solving complicated math problems is hard for everybody. Once you realize that, you will accept such an assignment as a challenge. You know there may be difficulties connected with a specific set of figures or certain situations. A setback is not necessarily due to your own error, but may be caused by *changing* conditions. You'll suc-ceed another time, when you are rested, having a better day, are better prepared, or have the proper tools available. If someone is constantly looking for mistakes within herself and thinks that con-ditions are unalterable, then it's probably her learned helplessness that is putting obstacles in her way.

On the basis of their past experience, some women think they are unable to achieve anything by their own efforts. They no longer rely on themselves. They hope for help from others or from prov-idence. They no longer believe in their own strength and compe-tence, and the patterns of dependency they have acquired leave them only one way out. They are forced to adapt to the wishes of others, and as a result, some of the joy and the feeling of being care-free goes out of their lives.

At the office, competent but helpless women wait to be discovered. There the fairy prince is called a mentor! Many women who feel stuck in a dead-end job are just waiting passively for him to come along. Instead of doing something, they hide their abilities and their ambitions. Yet when their superiors don't promote them, they feel hurt and disappointed. The sensible reaction would be to *fight* for support.

Helpless individuals have no faith in their skills and abilities. They worry that they have to depend on luck and coincidence to be successful. They don't give themselves credit for their accomplishments. They don't allow themselves to take any joy in their successes. When something goes wrong they immediately think they are at fault.

That has an effect on motivation and initiative. Helpless people suffer from inner lethargy, constant fatigue, burnout syndrome, sleeplessness, or aimless activity. They're convinced that they can't change anything and that they can't reach their goals on their own. They're afraid that they can't cope with their own lives. Yet very few people would describe themselves as helpless. Sure, they think they're at the mercy of all of life's adversities, but they believe the term *helpless* applies only to extreme situations and to other people.

Very few "helpless" women feel capable of taking charge of their own lives, of making the right decisions, and of supporting themselves. Such low self-assessments are not without consequences. Someone who expects to achieve nothing by herself is dependent on others. Women therefore think they have to concentrate all their energies on holding onto someone. They consider it an investment in their own future. Instead of investing their energy in getting organized, stabilizing their situation, and asserting themselves, they make poor compromises.

I'll show you why good girls don't get ahead, and I'll show you ways

- women who are resigned to being good can mount a joyful and lighthearted resistance

- women can eliminate the contradiction between goal-oriented action on their own behalf and maintaining congenial relations with other people.

I'll also clarify the position a New Woman must take in the conflict she faces between dependency and self-determination. Women *can* keep their lives in balance; they can achieve their rights without having a bad conscience. They can be strong without endangering their relationships and friendships.

Chapter 1

The
Great
Deception

.

Common Mental Traps

Lame Excuses

Many a "good" woman deceives herself: She thinks that a short-term benefit is sufficient compensation for "good" behavior; that, just to avoid a row, it's worth putting up with her husband's unwillingness to supervise the children's homework; that being taken out to dinner makes up for his not considering *her* suggestions for the family vacation; that a second car is sufficient compensation for giving up her wish to earn her own money. She thinks that the new winter coat her husband gave her makes up for his refusal to take care of the children when she goes to yoga class; that if she works overtime without complaining, she'll get a promotion.

But women are the losers in this swap. They disregard the fact that they've struck a bad bargain. In the end they're only forging another link in their own subjugation. There is a close connection between these seeming little victories and the fear of taking responsibility—the fear of showing one's true colors, of facing up to conflict or confrontation. Not only are "good" women afraid of taking responsibility for themselves, but they are also afraid to risk being unloved or unpopular for even a moment.

These self-imposed barriers indicate a reliance on old rules. They are lame excuses and hamper women in the fight for their rights.

We are blocked by false assumptions and *mental traps*. Our parents' and society's many precepts, both major and minor, demand our good behavior. Even small mental traps can have a major impact.

Anyone who violates social norms will experience sanctions; he or she will be threatened with ostracism or contempt. This leads to fears that in turn become mental traps.

Fears and anxieties function in ways we are rarely aware of. Take Freud's old example: He says that fear of snakes is displacement for fear of the penis. But at this point I don't want to talk about the relationship between sexual defense mechanisms and fears, but rather the effect of fear as a guardian of the status quo. Fear keeps us from taking action.

Don't Women Know What They Want?

Betty would like to fly to the Virgin Islands with her family for their next vacation. For the last three years she has longed to spend a couple of weeks there. Whenever she goes downtown, she brings back travel brochures, and shows them to her husband, Peter, and their nine-year-old daughter, Manuela. She's also bought several travel guides. Her proposal appeals to Peter, and Manuela is enthusiastic about the prospect of flying. But every year the three of them end up in a little cabin located on a farm in the mountains. Peter had already made the reservations the previous year while they were vacationing at the farm. And somehow or other it always turns out to be quite pleasant there. Nevertheless, Betty is becoming more and more disgruntled. She grouses and complains about having to cook and clean on vacation. Actually she would have preferred to book them on an all-inclusive tour.

But somehow something keeps Betty from simply going to a travel bureau and doing it. She suspects that Peter would really rather go to the mountains. Even though he always says he'd like to go elsewhere for a change, he never does anything about it. So now, after three years, Betty is still waiting for Peter to act. She interprets this as a secret rejection of her plan. She isn't aware that she herself is not doing anything either. She hasn't made any reservations because she doesn't want to steamroller Peter. If he wants to go, then *he* ought to make the reservations. After all, she has expressed her wish often enough. It's out of consideration for him that she has done without. Hasn't she said over and over again that she would like to fly to the Islands? She feels like a little child who keeps begging for something, but nobody pays her any heed—everyone says yes, but no one does anything. It didn't mean much that both of them said they'd like to fly to the Islands. Peter was the one who had to make the decision to really do it. He had to make the reservations.

Evidently in Betty's eyes what is valid for Peter doesn't apply to her. It doesn't occur to her that if *she* wants to go, *she* is the one who should make the reservations.

Helen had a similar experience. Weekends were usually a disaster. Her husband and the children would mumble agreement when she suggested what they might do, but nobody did anything. Then a few weeks ago Helen changed her approach. She would make a suggestion without worrying whether it would suit the others—and if there wasn't a clear "no" vote, she arranged the activity of her choice. So far they've all gone along and it's been fun. And even if, now and then, her husband or one of the children didn't want to join in, it wasn't the end of the world. In any case, she did what she enjoyed—whether it meant going to the swimming pool, a sauna, or on a hike.

Do you sense a hidden contradiction here? Is the word <u>egocentric</u> on the tip of your tongue?

Do you wonder: Am I steamrolling others? Perhaps you're having thoughts like: "You can't do that, you can't go over the heads of the others." If so, watch out; it shows that the "good girl" inside you is very powerful.

But to get back to Betty. She finally resolved to work out a detailed plan and, if there were no serious objections, to make the reservations. It worked. She figured out a tour, planned for sightseeing and time on the beach, put together a program with lots of variety, something for everybody. The family approved; only Peter, in an aside, reminded them that it would be very hot there.

Betty couldn't get that remark out of her head. Before she went to the travel bureau, she sat down in a café with a magazine to think the whole thing over in peace and quiet.

What if it really did get so hot there that you couldn't do anything? It would be her fault if the vacation turned into a fiasco. The longer she thought about it, the more horrible were the visions in her mind. So she decided she'd better not make reservations till the next day; at supper she'd carefully probe to find out if Peter really wanted to go. Her old doubts had taken hold of her again.

No Decision Is Ever One Hundred Percent Right

After all, even legislation is often determined by only a slim majority. It's hard to see that this applies to our private lives as well as to our jobs. Always act according to the same basic principle: First weigh the advantages and disadvantages, and then make a decision.

Are Women Only Soft and Gentle?

Women do their duty without resisting, without protest. They deny their aggressivity, even to themselves, because they are afraid of losing the affection of others. Any budding aggressions are immediately redirected against themselves or into another arena. A mother who is angry at her baby tries to lavish special care on it because a good mother must not be angry. She tortures herself with feelings of guilt and doesn't dare talk about the anger she feels toward the helpless little creature. The result is that her aggressions are turned inward, or the stored-up irritation unintentionally erupts against something or someone else.

Women suffer from migraine headaches and depressions more frequently than men. They feel worn-out, tired, and listless. Often there is a mountain of aggressivity concealed behind these complaints.

When female aggression is externalized, it often occurs in a very indirect, subtle way. Some women will snap at others from ambush; they make a nasty comment and beat a quick retreat.

Women are often jealous or envious. But they hide their aggressive feelings until, suddenly, like a volcano, these erupt unchecked. Of course, the outbursts are not unexpected because basically all of us, men and women, know that those who are suppressed will fight back someday, one way or another. The immediate provocation may be minor—a trifle that causes the cauldron to boil over.

Janet had returned to her job after a three-year leave of absence, a so-called family break. The three years had been anything but a break—certainly not from her family. She had made it possible for her husband, Gerald, to finish his studies in chemistry. Their twins, Annie and Lisa, had not been born at the most propitious time. After their birth, Janet had at first continued working full-time, but her hope that Gerald could manage both his studies and the children was soon shattered. So she resigned from her job as a lab supervisor. But she couldn't stop working entirely; after all, one of them had to support the family since Gerald had no income. So she worked the night shift; that brought in money, and during the day she could take on the household and the children.

It was okay—for a while. But again and again, frictions arose. Money was tight, Janet was exhausted, and Gerald was panicky about his exam. When he wanted a rest from cramming, he played basketball or went out with friends. This made Janet angry, but she thought she was being petty. After all, his examination was coming up soon—he needed to relax. Repeatedly she set aside her own wishes. There wasn't even time to be with her girlfriends; she had no chance to take a break and certainly none for serious conversations.

Finally Gerald finished his studies. True, he didn't find a job right away, but now she could go back to working full-time during the day; no more night shift, which in itself would make her feel better. He could take over the household until he found a good job. After all, the twins were already in kindergarten. Janet looked forward to working at her old job. And she was especially happy to be released from the housework.

But after only a few days it was clear that Gerald would not take on the housework by himself. When he went shopping, he came back with only half the items he was supposed to buy; so Janet had to stop off at the supermarket on her way home. Gerald did the laundry, but then Janet had to hang it up to dry when she came home in the evening and iron it the next day. At first she consoled herself with the thought that eventually things would work out, but her mood became more and more glum.

Although Janet was angry, she didn't admit to herself the intensity of the aggression she felt. After all, Gerald was trying. It wasn't his fault that he forgot so many things. He had more important matters to think about. Besides, Janet decided, it was really *her* fault: She had spoiled him and had mothered him. Gerald had never had a chance to learn how to manage a household. When they first met, he was living in a one-room apartment, taking his dirty laundry to his mother, and most of the time eating his meals there too. When Janet moved in with him, she took care of him. Lovingly she cooked for him and set the table for romantic suppers and cozy breakfasts.

Although Janet was annoyed that Gerald didn't try harder to find a job, she figured that maybe he needed time off after his studies.

She thought she had no right to have aggressive feelings. And she was afraid to risk losing Gerald's affection if she were to make demands on him now. She wasn't sure he would continue to love her if she were to make life less convenient for him.

Janet was walking into two traps at the same time: First, she thought she had no right to have aggressive feelings. *Good girls don't get angry.* Second, she thought she had to earn her husband's affection by providing services to him. *Good girls make sacrifices for others.* "Love means . . . washing his socks."

Janet thinks that if she were to let out her anger, Gerald would leave her. For years she had been *taming* her *bad* qualities, controlling her aggression for fear of losing him. And in some way she has been afraid all along that he would eventually see through her; he might find out that she isn't as nice as she always acts. And then he would leave her; of that, she is sure. She knows how much he treasures her amiability, her kindness, because they've often talked about how unpleasant his friends' wives are. His disparaging remarks about the other wives kept ringing in her ears: "When the study group meets at Peter's house, his wife, Monica, doesn't even offer us a beer or a snack. She just keeps griping about having to clean up after we leave." In contrast they all enjoyed coming to study at Gerald's house.

Or take Ingrid, who often saddled them with her six-month-old baby so that she could go to the movies with her girlfriends while her husband and his friends were studying together.

Janet wasn't like that at all. She made things pleasant for her husband and his ambitious friends. And she loved it when she overheard them criticize the other women. But now she was well on the way to being just like those women.

Janet decided to have a talk with the other two wives. They told her that they hadn't always been so "inconsiderate" and that even now they often felt guilty when they followed their own interests. But they had managed to get their husbands to take them more seriously. Having clearly shown their anger gained them respect.

Janet resolved to object more frequently, to accept less of the workload. From now on she would not avoid conflicts. *Being nice and helpful hadn't worked.* She was not going to be intimidated by rules made by others. This is certainly a difficult course to take, but it's the first step to self-determination. Janet has had it "up to here" with decisions made for her by others, especially when the others put pressure on her.

It is hard to predict Gerald's response to her new attitude. Maybe he'll pull back, get angry, or maybe he'll be glad. If he gives signs of rejection and indicates he wants a separation, it will be primarily a reaction to an unfamiliar situation that he didn't expect and for which he's not prepared. Janet will have to stay calm if he blows his stack. After all, he is suddenly being confronted by demands he's not accustomed to. So he may react by feeling furious, helpless, sad, or offended. Many men become anxious when a woman shows her strong side. Their reactions are unpredictable. It's important to know that their behavior is a consequence of surprise and confusion. The woman must not be frightened by it.

If you want to give up the old behavior pattern, you'll have to pay attention to the following:

Don't be afraid of your own anger!
Don't be afraid of your partner's anger!
Being nice doesn't get you anywhere!

Sylvia was seething with anger. It was after midnight, and she had just come home from her computer-course graduation party. All the lights in the house were on, and as she opened the door, her two children, Oliver, seven, and Jessica, four, charged toward her. More than anything she wanted to bawl them out, but first she picked up the little girl in her arms and stroked Oliver's hair. Just before rage overwhelmed her, an inner voice whispered, "You *could* have come home earlier."

Robert was sitting in the living room calmly playing chess with Eric, one of their neighbors. Apparently he hadn't even noticed the chaos in the bathroom and in the kitchen. Sylvia's face was flushed with anger. She scolded Robert, furiously reproaching him. Just for once, couldn't he have put the children quietly to bed; did he have to invite Eric to play chess tonight of all nights; he should have played with the children, should have read them stories, should have made sure that they went to bed on time. Suddenly she realized that she was yelling, and she felt petty. The whole scene was embarrassing. What would Eric think of her? She had stormed into the living room like a shrieking banshee. Ashamed, she mumbled, "I'm sorry," and prepared to put the children to bed.

If you want to bail out of this thought pattern, remember:

She was right to have been angry.
She shouldn't feel bad because she was upset.
It's appropriate to show anger.
Nothing awful will happen because she was furious.

Many women are afraid of their own anger because angry women often make other people feel helpless. A man in a towering rage is socially accepted—everybody knows that any normal guy has to blow his top every once in a while. A woman, on the other hand, is generally expected to be affable. People are astonished when she really flies off the handle. And since women in a towering rage are a rare occurrence, no one knows how to deal with them. Most women are actually afraid of themselves when they feel anger. They don't know how they will act once they give free rein to their rage.

By doing the following short exercise, you can find out what might happen if you were to get very angry: Imagine, in detail, a situation that would make you furious, and visualize the consequences.

You could also sit down with a woman friend and take turns describing what might happen if you were to get really mad. After a few minutes you would undoubtedly realize that your fears of the terrible things that might happen are unfounded.

Because a woman is afraid of her own anger, she is often completely unable to sense her feelings of rage. Aggressive feelings are diverted and turned against herself. They express themselves in tiredness, a fixed smile, headaches, listlessness, insomnia, depression, etc.

There were many nights when Sylvia couldn't sleep, but usually she didn't realize that her anger was causing the problem. One night after she had had a fight with Robert, it dawned on her just what was wrong. When she couldn't fall asleep, she began to suspect that maybe she was *often* angry but wasn't really aware of it anymore. She resolved to track down her anger.

Now when she lies in bed and can't sleep, she thinks: "Today I was angry because . . ." and she lists every tiny annoyance. After a few minutes she goes a step further; for each annoyance she adds a sentence describing what would have happened if she had reacted angrily or simply acted on impulse.

Soon Sylvia could sense when she was getting angry. After a few weeks she dared to do something about it. She began on a small scale, with people whom she trusted. She told a girlfriend that she was mad at her because she had kept her waiting in a coffee bar for three quarters of an hour. When she was upset with Robert, she didn't keep her anger to herself anymore. She got mad when he didn't keep the children off her back while she was working at the computer. She let her mother know she was displeased that she wasn't willing to baby-sit occasionally for her grandchildren. She permitted herself to snap at Robert when he didn't want to do anything on weekends.

Often There Is Hidden Strength in Anger.

Are Women Really Weak?

Most women are stronger than they think. They see themselves as weak, dependent creatures who need the protection of a strong man.

Cecile has a two-year-old son, Alexander. Ever since he was born she has been suffering from anxieties so profound, she often cannot leave the house. She no longer goes shopping, and driving the car or going on vacation is out of the question. She got married to get away from her parents. She did not plan to get pregnant. To be honest, she never really made any decisions. Everything just happened, and in the end she just gave up. Now she can't go on. She can't stand being afraid, night and day. She longs to be happy again, to be able to move about freely, and she decides to go into therapy. Quite methodically, she learns to leave the house, to visit women friends, to drive the car. Next she asks herself what she really wants, and two years later she follows her wishes. Once she realizes that she no longer wants to lead *his* life, she separates from her husband.

Cecile had been afraid of her own strength. Her fear kept her from becoming rebellious and from recognizing all the things she didn't like about their life together and their relationship.

Should a Furious Woman Be Denounced as a Raging Hysteric?

People often label strength as hysteria, as acting in the heat of passion, or showing a lack of self-control. When Fay Weldon* describes the life and loves of her "she-devil," women smile knowingly at the fiendish reactions of her heroine. No doubt women consider it logical that she should blow her top—she gets her children and pets out of the house and then destroys the symbols of her oppression by letting all the household appliances overheat until the entire house burns to the ground. Then she drops off the kids at the house of her husband's mistress, and at last she's free.

You probably could imagine a more successful denouement to this story than that the heroine is merely trying to teach her husband a lesson. She could become really independent, could set goals that would make her self-sufficient—but in any case, the beginning is spectacular.

Why Do Women Always Have to Be Beautiful?

When women become furious they pose a threat, not only to men, but also to themselves. Their faces turn ugly when they get angry.

---

*Weldon, Fay, *The Life and Loves of a She-Devil.* New York: Pantheon Books, 1983.

And so they prefer to hide their anger. Their partner says, "Look in the mirror. When you carry on like that, you look horrible." He's certainly sowing on fertile ground; quickly she tries to improve her looks with a smile. "There," he says, "that's better!"

She doesn't care that smiling at this point undermines her power to assert herself. Beauty is more important than self-respect. She wants to be liked even if she loses face. She smiles, belittles herself, gives in before it's too late, before he recognizes her hidden "ugliness." How could she let herself go like that? The effect of her smile on him is astonishing. He gives in, consoles her, and then goes right ahead putting *his* suggestions into action. He's done it. He doesn't have to be afraid of her anymore.

Women, the beautiful gender. This is the snare in every situation wherein women might discover their assertiveness, independence, and self-esteem. The price they would have to pay would be their femininity, their beauty. And so women denigrate themselves by putting on a smiling mask.

As a result they are not taken seriously; they cannot present themselves. They give up power and independence.

For a long time Pamela had waited for the go-ahead from her boss to attend a seminar about a new computer program. It was supposed to start this Saturday and run for ten consecutive Saturdays, a convenient time, especially because Dave could take care of their daughter, Stefanie, age three, on Saturdays. Full of enthusiasm, she tells Dave that things were finally working out. She assumes he would be pleased too. After all, he knows how important the additional training is to her. His comment throws her for a loop: "Good for you, but I hope you've asked your mother whether she has all those Saturdays free to baby-sit." Pamela is struck dumb; the words stick in her throat. What's her mother got to do with it? Dave points out tersely that he wants to play tennis on Saturdays. He needs it to relax. He is happy that he finally was able to pry his pal Peter away from his wife to play with him. There's absolutely no way he is going to give that up.

Pamela flips out completely. She panics when she sees her chance to take the training course vanish. Besides, her boss would consider her capricious. For months she's been pestering him, and now she chickens out when it really matters—just like a woman. A red-faced Pamela screams at Dave in anger. The tears smear her mascara, her voice cracks. Dave pulls out all the stops: "You ought to see yourself now, how hideous you look when you make such a hysterical scene." Pamela runs out of the room, goes into the bathroom, and admits defeat. Somehow he is right. He works hard all week long, and she wants to saddle him with their kid on Saturdays— that really isn't very considerate. She vacillates between calling off the training course or once again asking her mother to pitch in and help, and the feeling that she'd rather run away, away from her husband who always lets her down.

Pamela is trapped. She wants Dave to acknowledge her career ambitions, to support them, to respect them. But as soon as she talks to him seriously to argue her case and, if need be, to force him to keep his promises, she feels like a helpless little girl. She stamps her foot petulantly, cries, and completely loses control. No wonder he wins. In a paternal, composed voice he condescendingly explains his view of things and then does what *he* wants. At the end of these discussions, which occur again and again, she always feels like leaving him. And at the same time, she also wants to please him. She thinks she's losing her marbles. She wants to get away but she's afraid he will leave her. Maybe that's the reason she doesn't want him to see her looking so ugly and puffy-eyed from crying. Her fear of being deserted is stronger than her desire to run away.

But it isn't always profound fears that keep a woman from living up to her potential. Often seemingly harmless stereotypes keep her thoughts and actions within narrow boundaries.

Do Strong Women Have to Be Lonely?

Even a concept like independence can have negative connotations and thereby lead into a mental trap. Often we equate independence with loneliness. And so a typical but deceptive association is created: *"Someone who is independent is also lonely."* Fear of being alone becomes a treacherous snare. That is why some women try to make themselves indispensable. They want to be needed. Leading a lonely life is the worst thing they can imagine. They sacrifice themselves so as not to be alone; they smile, and in spite of that, they still feel an inner loneliness. There are numerous mental traps, but the linking of independence and loneliness, in particular, gives many women a hard time.

The Idea That Independence Makes You Lonely Is Wrong!

On the contrary, independence makes it possible to have creative, relaxed, and open relationships. Only someone who is *not* dependent on other people can decide freely with whom she wants to be involved and how. Only autonomous *and* independent individuals can live together as equals.

This does not mean that one cannot help the other or that they will not try to please each other. But it must always be based on one's own, free decision. And many women seem to have lost sight of that. Blinded by the worry that they won't be loved, they orient themselves more by the wishes and needs of others than by their own. They are afraid to hurt others, and withdraw before they even know what they *themselves* want. At best they think that they agree with all the things they do out of love or consideration for others, and they cannot understand their own growing dissatisfaction. They see themselves as ungrateful and moody.

A

A woman ought to take time out when she feels she can't stand herself anymore or when, for no apparent reason, she is in a bad mood. Try to find what your personal mental traps are. Ask yourself:

What would I do if I could make this decision independently, by myself? What would I like to do? Do I want to do it by myself or with somebody else?

Do Women Have to Be Mothers?

A good mother puts her own needs last.

Children always come first. Children are the most important thing in a woman's life.

Motherhood is the clearest proof that one belongs to the female gender. The reverse conclusion, that a woman without a child isn't a real woman, is first of all illogical, and second, pretty silly. Nevertheless, it seems to influence even successful professional women's thinking.

Peggy, a biochemist, had a happy and candid relationship with her husband; they worked in the same laboratory and found talking about their work interesting and stimulating—until Peggy reached her thirty-fifth birthday and thought that she had to decide within the next few years whether she wanted to have a child. Like air seeping out of a punctured tire, the lightheartedness escaped from their lives. To grow old without a child suddenly seemed to be wrong. They talked of nothing else but her getting pregnant. Within a year Peggy conceived. After the birth of the child she stayed home, and for three years she was the world's happiest woman with the world's sweetest baby. Unfortunately, after another two years she couldn't get her job back because no laboratory would even think of hiring someone who had been out of the field for five years. After that Peggy was the world's unhappiest woman, full of anger and despair because she had risked her entire future for the wonderful time spent with her baby. Finally she did find a job, but clearly it did not entail the challenges she was accustomed to. She was obviously overqualified and didn't feel anywhere near the satisfaction she had found in her former job.

Another woman told me that her doctor, whom she had consulted about her general feeling of malaise, had suggested, "Why don't you have a couple of kids. It will make you feel like a real woman, and you won't have any more complaints."

Motherhood and a career are splendidly compatible because we believe a woman who is a "stay-at-home mom" may run the risk of expecting too much of her child, tying it to her apron strings, or suffocating it with love.

A woman who has no serious desire to have children, but who believes, nonetheless, that she cannot do without this biological testimony to her femininity, may say: "I feel incomplete, as though I'm missing something important." The words reflect her inner conflict. Conforming to societal pressure, she becomes pregnant, and very soon she feels imprisoned. One woman who was suffering a great deal in her role as mother told me the only reason she had a child was "because suddenly all my friends were having children." Many women become mothers without having seriously decided they want a child. Yet they never considered the alternative—life without a child.

Does a Woman Need a Husband?

A wedding dress conceals all heartache!
Girls don't need a good education. They get married!

Many mothers, fathers, and daughters are still obsessed with the idea that every woman will one day arrive at a point in her life when she'll decide to get married and have children. This implies that she'll find a man who will take care of her. No matter what educational credentials and how much independence this woman may have achieved, her goal remains to win a man who has maximum potency in every respect. To assure this result, there are certain clear rules that turn women into small, harmless, good creatures.

Unfortunately, even today one of the main objectives in a woman's life is to catch a man. The higher the man's position, the higher will be the woman's too. In a TV commercial, a friendly woman is heard to say: "As a dentist's wife . . ." Just the fact that her husband is a dentist is supposed to testify to her expertise and qualify her to give a testimonial. She herself doesn't need the credentials. She has proved herself competent in that she snagged a successful man. The title "wife" seems to be the only title that women truly value. They're even willing to give up their own name, although the law says they don't have to. Even women who are successful in their careers enhance their standing by having a *steady partner.* Their own success is insignificant without a husband.

But the status of "wife" comes at a price. True, unlike most men, she doesn't have to study and cram for a professional degree, but she does have to be prepared to serve and be subservient, to do the dirty work for others, and always be happy playing second fiddle. Spunky girls may be admired, but conventional folk wisdom says it's the innocent ones, the "good" ones, the modest and obedient ones, who get married.

The husband (not the wife) is the one who has to go out into the hostile world!

A wife may choose to work, a husband must!

Today one can still see women who for years were active in the feminist movement being "good wives and mothers," cleaning and polishing their houses and waving good-bye to their husbands as they go off to work in the mornings to earn the family income. Even women who feel solidarity with the feminist movement stumble into mental traps that suggest they still need a man, even if only to ensure their standard of living.

Women work independently, they travel alone, and they follow their own interests until they enter into a steady relationship and become mothers. At first they think they can still hold on to their freedom, but in the end the old role clichés sneak in. It's true that women today argue more often with their spouses about the fair distribution of housework, but in the end they feel responsible for the smooth running of the household and the care of the children, even if nowadays some men will clean the stairs, vacuum the carpet, and take care of the kids. When it comes to getting a baby-sitter, it's the woman who does it; if household help is needed, it's the wife who tries to find someone; and when her husband goes shopping, she makes up the shopping list.

However, when important decisions have to be made, such as buying a car or moving to a new house or apartment, then he calls the shots.

⚠

Imagine that you are gradually going to suggest to your partner that he share in some of the following responsibilities:

Give him a list of baby-sitters and their telephone numbers and ask him to call and make arrangements with one of them. Remind him several times, even if you feel strange doing it, that it's his job to get the baby-sitter.

Help him make up the shopping list a few times until he's familiar with how it's done.

Now, <u>you</u> take responsibility for some of the <u>big</u> decisions.

Make a list of your criteria for buying a car, and suggest two models he can choose from.

Imagine that you are asking him to move to another city for the sake of <u>your</u> career.

I Can't Take Care of Myself on My Own!

This mental trap may also be concealed in such notions as:

Having a husband enhances one's self-esteem. I feel more secure, stronger, decisive, when there's a man in my life. My abilities are more readily recognized because I'm a married woman. I'm taken more seriously than I would be as a single woman. A husband keeps you from having to hold down a job of your own and from being harassed by others. It's like having life insurance.

Jennifer's example shows how effectively women can talk themselves into believing that they need a man; her mental trap was: "I can't manage alone."

Jennifer is a translator. She has been married to Tim for fifteen years. They have three children: Nina, fifteen, Oliver, thirteen, and Sabrina, nine. Five years ago they bought a house with a garden on the outskirts of a small town. With the birth of each child, Jennifer never took more than the standard maternity leave. However, after

Sabrina's birth, she decided to take half a year off, but after only three months she went back to work because her firm needed a vacation substitute. For quite some time she worked only part-time, but as the children needed her less, she started working more hours.

Jennifer loved their house; she enjoyed puttering in her garden as soon as she got home. She had been a member of a political organization for years, and shortly after their move, some friends in the local party asked if she wanted to become more active. She'd always been interested in politics, and getting involved would give her a chance to make new contacts. Besides, she was flattered to have been asked.

Jennifer was competent, and on top of her job, she managed the household, she raised her children, and she was enthusiastic about her political involvement—she is a strong and self-confident woman. It really looked as though she could have a career in politics. She had never expected to have a chance like this.

But suddenly everything became unclear. Jennifer's husband insisted that they sell the house and move to a nearby city, just as her political involvement was beginning to pay off. He said it was for financial reasons, but his explanation seemed flimsy.

Even though Jennifer knew this was just a pretext, she gave in. She didn't really know what was behind his decision, and she was afraid to ask questions, so she agreed. They sold the house, and she gave up her hopes for a political career.

At first glance it's amazing that her husband's blackmail succeeded. Jennifer and Tim hadn't felt really close for a long time. They continued to live together more out of inertia than anything else. Up to now there hadn't been any pressing reason for a separation, and also there were the children. . . .

Still Jennifer found herself suddenly holding on to her marriage. She was convinced that she needed Tim. She was quite sure she couldn't be successful without a husband.

She believed that as a single mother, she wouldn't make it, either at her job or in politics. She saw her status of married woman as more important than her political involvement and her competence, thereby devaluing her work. Her abilities, she thought, were worth less than her image as wife and mother. She was afraid that the other people who worked in her political party would not appreciate her and her abilities if she didn't have a husband. And she thought that her political abilities were only good enough for "a small town." Ultimately she gave up her own career because of her fear of being "without a husband." She didn't have enough self-confidence to think that she could manage her life alone—even though conditions for that were optimal.

Jennifer didn't know she had options. She was attached to her house, and yet it didn't occur to her to get information about financing that would have made it possible for her to keep the house. She had always taken care of all the family's banking and the mortgage payments. A talk with someone at her bank would have shown her that it was quite feasible for her to maintain the house. But she stubbornly clung to the idea that she didn't stand a chance of ensuring that she and her children would have a roof over their heads. At the threat of being left without a husband, all her competence seemed to have evaporated.

A woman's fear of not being able to support herself is deep-seated, even if she's been taking care of her family for many years.

Jennifer knew that up to now she'd taken care of everything herself, but she was terribly worried that she wouldn't have any security without Tim around. Even her own practical experience wasn't enough to ward off the old ingrained mental trap:

A woman needs a man. A woman always needs someone to encourage her, to rescue her, and to help her.

Moreover, women have a great fear of losing face. A deserted woman is a woman with a defect. And just the general feeling that something isn't quite right if you live alone forces some women to give in and make decisions that are contrary to their own wishes and feelings.

Jennifer thought that she could keep her husband by giving in to him. *He* wanted to move to the city, but *she* was the one who found their new apartment and hired the movers. *She* guided the children through their new school routines, organized get-acquainted parties for the older ones and afternoon play dates for the youngest. *She* did everything so that they would feel comfortable and happy. *She* made it easier for the children to leave their old home, and now she pretends that she is satisfied with the move so that Tim won't feel guilty. And after all that, *she* still thinks she isn't capable of assuring her livelihood and of managing her life with the children!

She hopes that being good will save her marriage. For that she will give up everything that is important to her and would allow her to get ahead in life. She resigns herself to her supposed destiny and is blind to other paths available to her.

Self-Denial Is Not a Long-Term Solution.

Perhaps in a subtle way Jennifer will take her revenge, the way many women do. She'll waste horrendous amounts of money in order to reconcile herself to her fate. First, she'll take a few days off, flying somewhere to recover from all the strain—maybe two weeks at a resort with a girlfriend. She'll buy new furniture: "It's hardly worthwhile taking the old junk along." She'll often go out evenings, explaining that she doesn't want to grow stodgy sitting at home just because she can't be politically active anymore. The conflicts were programmed. Jennifer didn't complain to Tim, but she let out her anger elsewhere.

She believed that she had acted in a reasonable and well thought-out way. But she failed to see that she had not paid attention to her own needs. She forced herself to remain calm and didn't fulfill her real needs, trying to find vicarious gratification in substitutes. Women haven't learned that they must first find out what they themselves want. They don't think about what *their* needs are and the misgivings and fears that keep them from going their own way. Perhaps if she had reflected a little, Jennifer might have realized that her success in politics, her work with her party friends, and the feeling of having set something in motion were all essential to her contentment. She might have sensed that she had drawn important benefits from her work, namely self-confirmation and self-respect. She carelessly gave up both in exchange for the questionable image of being a married woman.

Jennifer's mental trap consisted in believing that she needed the label "married woman." For that she sacrificed her self-respect.

But she also expected to gain an advantage: She would not have to risk facing challenges seriously. She was spared the danger of failure by her husband's decision to move, but she was also kept from having a career and all that it might have meant to her.

In the past, Jennifer proved that she could be independent and self-reliant. She had made important decisions, not only for herself but for her entire family, including her parents, sisters, and brothers. She had taken care of financial matters, had kept a cool head in crises, and had acted decisively when somebody was sick. She was able to: *earn her own living, sell her political and organizational skills, convince people and win them over to her side.*

She had amply demonstrated all this. Neither her husband nor anyone else had a hand in her accomplishments. Now it's Jennifer's turn to recognize all this. She must have faith in herself and her abilities. She must convince herself that she can earn recognition and respect without a husband. And she must demand recognition for her achievements.

⚠

Is the problem of not daring to take the first step familiar to you? Are you often much too quick to give up on things that are important to you? Do you act against your own interests? Then you must learn to respect yourself. Your feeling of self-worth must not depend on whether you have a husband. Only the woman who believes in herself can convince others of her worth.

Chapter 2

Mental Traps
in the Workplace

.

"Helpfulness Will Be Rewarded"

This rule comes in several variants:

- Eagerness to work will be rewarded
- Restraint will be recognized
- Modesty pays

Women believe that in addition to competence and industriousness, smiling and being pleasant are prerequisites for career success. In spite of their own experiences, they cling to the idea that self-sacrifice is the best way to convince someone of their accomplishments.

For the past year Sandra has been working in a law office. A lawyer, she hopes to become a partner soon. She works late into the night and offers to pitch in whenever a senior partner is handing out extra work. Long ago when she was a little girl, her grandfather told her, "Always be helpful and good, and don't ever become discouraged." Sandra took that to heart; the advice became her motto. She got her law degree by working hard, refusing to become discouraged, even helping her fellow students when they were running out of steam. Getting the job in the law office was also due to her own efforts. She demonstrated her helpfulness when she was working there as an intern. And she continues to show that she is eager to work. As a student she had a job as a typist and her typing speed is phenomenal. She will take over for the legal secretaries when they want to go home on time but haven't yet finished an important file. She wants to show that she isn't above doing menial work. The secretaries are all women; she wants them to like her. Besides, she feels women have to stick together. She works till midnight and on weekends without grumbling, typing legal documents and doing routine jobs.

Every time one of the senior partners asks her to come into his office, she expects him to offer her a partnership. After all, her work has been perfect and she is always ready to help. But something has gone awry. A colleague who was hired after she joined the firm has already gone through the preliminary negotiations for a partnership. Sandra cannot understand what went wrong. True, the colleague also works hard, but she pitches in considerably more; she does more overtime than he, and she always jumps in when one of the secretaries doesn't show up; *he* always thinks himself above that.

Now he is making outrageous demands in his negotiations for a partnership, and it looks as though, in the process, she's going to be left out in the cold. They're certainly not going to offer partnerships to two lawyers. It's dawning on Sandra that it isn't being good that leads to success, but boldness and audacity. In any case, that strategy seems to work for men.

She never gets the partnership. Sandra made a typically feminine error in judgment. She thought that to achieve success, it was enough to be competent, hardworking, and pleasant. In her mind she set up an unspoken contract: She would invest her readiness to work hard, her industriousness, her willingness to make sacrifices, and her modesty; in exchange for which—after a reasonable period of time—she would get the partnership.

But her calculation couldn't possibly work because the other "contracting parties," the partners, didn't know anything about the agreement. Sandra had forgotten one essential factor: She has to make her demands clear, to say what she wants and what she expects. She must negotiate terms that will state precisely what she must accomplish in order to become a partner. What Sandra considers rash and outrageous are merely specific and unequivocal demands. This is the only correct strategy for getting what one wants. It works for women as well as for men. One thing is certain: A woman who does clerical work cannot become a partner. It would have been a more adroit move on her part to show that she could line up good temporary typists, or that she could inspire the secretaries to work harder, take less time off, and occasionally stay late.

There's no doubt that Sandra is a competent lawyer. And competence is an essential building block toward success, but it isn't the only one. Sandra is not aware of the rules that govern the business world:

⚠

- **Concentrate your energies on potentially successful projects.**
- **Set yourself long-term goals and don't lose sight of them.**
- **Don't waste time wondering what others think of you.**
- **Make clear agreements and demands.**

Instead of following these rules, Sandra was a "good girl"!

She frittered away her energies taking on tasks that could have been done by less qualified personnel instead of working purposefully on cases that would demonstrate her legal abilities.

Although Sandra aimed for a partnership, she lost sight of her goal. She got bogged down in trivia, typed legal documents, and took on routine office work that distracted her from important high-visibility courtroom trials.

She covered for others so they would like her. By doing so she unknowingly gave up her chances for professional success. Worrying that the secretaries would think her arrogant, she came down to their level and relieved them of some of their workload, instead of using them to help her.

Sandra had come to no clear agreement with the senior partners about the work she would have to produce to be eligible for a partnership. Nor had she agreed on a definite time frame in which negotiations were to take place.

Patiently she just waited for the senior partner to come to her with an offer, instead of asking for a partnership.

Many women think along similar lines. They feel they shouldn't consider themselves above doing "simple" tasks, or even to work without pay in order to demonstrate their ability.

However, career stumbling blocks may also lie at home: Bridget owns a small boutique that is doing well. In spite of her ten-hour workdays, she does the cleaning both at home and in the shop. She is too embarrassed to hire a cleaning woman because her neighbors and friends might think she's putting on airs.

Heather, a psychologist, has worked pro bono for two years in a rehab clinic for drug addicts. When a part-time job was posted, she thought she would be hired. She wasn't. Why should the clinic pay someone who is willing to work for nothing?

"I Have to Do What Is Expected of Me"

This mental trap also can have different versions. The variations listed below can lead into the trap "Being good will be rewarded":

- Do exactly what you are told, then you can't do anything wrong.
- Speak only when you are asked to speak. Hold back and keep your ideas and opinions to yourself; then you won't make a fool of yourself.
- Don't be brash! Wait patiently till you're discovered.

Fairy tales send strong messages to women. Remember Cinderella? For a long time she did exactly what her evil stepmother ordered her to do. She was submissive and worked hard. She never complained. But her silent submission was not rewarded. Only when she finally disobeyed, left the house, got herself beautiful clothes, and went to the royal ball against her stepmother's orders did something positive happen. Success came only after Cinderella stopped being passive and good.

You can take this as a general rule: Women who serve devotedly and submissively will get no recognition or reward for it. It's much too convenient to have someone around who's willing to do the dirty work. There is no reason to promote her.

Women must stop degrading themselves by acting as maids. They have to disobey orders and prohibitions that force them to perform tasks that lead nowhere. I frequently encounter meek Cinderella types among working women. For instance:

Christine, who is a graphic artist, has clever ideas, works carefully, and invests a lot of her free time learning new computer-aided design techniques. Three years ago, fresh out of school, she began working for a large agency. She had excellent references and an impressive portfolio and hoped at the time to advance rapidly in her chosen career. Today, three years later, Christine is angry because she is still doing the same preliminary work, assisting others in the agency. Now and then she completes some small assignments, but she is never given demanding projects of her own. She is still convinced she has the necessary skills, and several times she has indicated to her boss that she would like to take on more complex assignments.

Her superiors are quite willing to admit that she executes her assignments carefully and exactly. Many of the ideas she submits are praised. And yet it's always the same co-workers, usually men, who get the good jobs. In telling me this, Christine emphasizes that she always sticks to the guidelines; she does her assignments perfectly. Her colleagues, on the other hand, are unreliable, she says; they change the guidelines and use their own ideas. Often the results have very little to do with what the clients asked for. And yet the clients seem satisfied.

Christine once brought up the subject at lunch with one of her colleagues, a man who is very painstaking in his work. He described to her how he tries to gauge what the client really wants. The clients' suggestions might be ideas they've seen used elsewhere or something they came up with themselves. They're really hoping that an expert can turn their suggestions into something better, something exceptional. A zippy, original idea is usually more important to the client than the flattery of seeing his own amateurish ideas used. Christine has some flashy ideas; there are many things she would have changed in clients' concepts, but up to now she's missed every chance to introduce her "daring" ideas. She hasn't even made suggestions.

The talk at lunch with her colleague proves to be a turning point in her career. She decides to take her ideas more seriously. Hesitantly, at first with small projects, she begins to give her own concepts priority.

She presents every client with a proposal based on what he suggested, but she also submits her own alternative approach. Most of the clients agree with her ideas, often enthusiastically. Her boss notices that Christine is doing more independent work. She is given more challenging jobs and more important clients.

She still pays attention to the clients' wishes. But first she asks herself what her own approach would be, and from that she develops suggestions for each project. Only if the client doesn't like her approach at all does she implement his idea. Christine now understands that employees who do their assignments reliably and predictably, who punctually deliver exactly what is expected of them, are absolutely essential for the smooth functioning of any enterprise. They are likely to keep their secure positions forever.

But those who get ahead are the ones who show distinctive individuality. They may rub some people the wrong way, but they certainly won't stay at the same job. If more promising projects are available at another firm, they'll switch.

﹍sful people loudly and clearly present their own ideas, ex-
ir wishes, and make demands. They make it clear that
nt to take on extraordinary assignments.

"Only Someone Who's Exhausted Has Really Accomplished Something!"

This mental trap has numerous variations:

If it just drops into my lap, it's not worth anything.
I'm embarrassed to let others work for me.
I have to prove that I can take it.
I'm not too high and mighty to do "menial" work.

Frequently women consider themselves arrogant or exploitative when others work for them. They feel they themselves ought to take care of difficult, time-consuming tasks, and they load themselves down with things they "couldn't expect others to do." Only after they've worked really hard and "gotten their hands dirty" do they permit themselves to reap the laurels of success—no gain without pain. Tasks that are pleasant and promising or less strenuous are a luxury and not worth much. Women who accomplish their work without feeling that it's a burden, or, even worse, who do it with pleasure, often have the sense that they haven't really been working. If a task is easy to do, they think it's of little value. This happens quite often when you become very familiar with your job. As soon as your work turns routine and is no longer connected with strenuous preparation and stressful doubt, you get the feeling that you haven't really accomplished anything—and that you haven't earned the money you're being paid. You didn't have to work that hard, so you're getting the reward without having noticeably exerted yourself. That attitude can't turn out well.

Anne writes for a daily newspaper. She's been doing this for twelve years and she knows her field. She works purposefully and quickly. And because she writes well and always meets deadlines, she usually gets exciting assignments. The job is a cinch for her, but she isn't happy. She has the feeling that something isn't right. Her colleagues grunt and groan; they're all done in at the end of the day. She's the only one who feels fine. She begins to suspect that she's not working hard enough.

Anne can't seem to enjoy her success and her professionalism.

Instead of being glad that she has her job so well in hand and feels good about her work, she doesn't believe in herself.

As they gain professional experience, many women lose their sense of accomplishment. They think their work isn't worth anything and they're afraid they're not doing enough. They measure good work by the physical and mental strain it brings, not by the perfect execution of a task, their creative input, or recognition from others. The consequence is that women work until they're exhausted. For them, it's not the satisfactory completion of a project that matters, but rather the degree of exhaustion they feel. Also, women often suffer from burnout because they usually set their standards too high and therefore enjoy their successes only moderately.

Many women still have to learn that:

Work that is easily done is valuable too.

It is precisely the woman who does her work with professional proficiency and seemingly without great effort who has accomplished something.

Chapter 3

Fear of Power

·

Power means using every opportunity, no matter what its source, to assert one's own will within a social relationship, even in the face of opposition from others.

MAX WEBER

Women renounce power, and that helps stabilize traditional social hierarchies. Unwittingly, women end up helping to keep fossilized power structures intact.

The word *power* has negative connotations for many people. They associate it with corruption, ruthlessness, and exploitation. Most women don't want power; they don't want to impose their opinions on others. But in many subtle ways, they do so anyway while denying it, even to themselves. They are afraid of their own power. They're afraid that no one will love a powerful woman.

There are some notions—mental traps—that, even though they have never been proved valid, influence women's actions. These prejudices, which reveal the fear women have of using power, set up roadblocks in a woman's path to attaining power. Here are examples of such traps:

Using power makes you lonely.
Always go by what you have been told.
Someone with power exploits others.
Women can't take on responsibility.
Don't use professional or social connections to get ahead.
Women are the power behind the throne.

You have to fight constantly to keep your power.
Good girls don't compete.
Names and titles aren't worth a hoot.
People with power have sold their souls.
I can't take any risks.
Power makes you unpopular.
Whoever exalts himself will be humbled.

Will Power Make Me Lonely?

Success and power are closely related. And doesn't everyone want to be successful in his or her own way? Often, the greater the desire for success, the greater also the desire for power. At work, reaching for success and power is called climbing the ladder, but women especially are afraid of loneliness if they take this path. Most women think it is a path for men only. Men are the tough solitary fighters, admired as much as they are pitied. According to female logic, the solitary man deliberately decides to go his solitary way. But it's different for the so-called powerful woman. She controls her hunger for power, and at crucial junctures she decides to take the more circuitous route, not the steep, direct one. When in doubt, she chooses friendship, cooperation, and social contact.

She doesn't understand that power and success on the one hand and loneliness on the other have nothing to do with each other. True, there are many examples of powerful *and* lonely men who *seem* to prove that power and loneliness are correlates. And it really is difficult to recognize that such men do *not* prove that loneliness goes hand in hand with power. For all too often, men, once they have power, occupy their time with struggles for status; they give up quality time with their families and leisure activities with friends. With this behavior they actually *create* their own loneliness. Men are just as much constrained by male structures as women are by female ones. Women do not have to adopt *this* particular male lifestyle in order to be successful and powerful. Nevertheless, they set up obstacles to their own success and power because they don't dare explore new avenues.

Some men and many women will put down a strong woman fighting to make it alone. They see her as someone who's been left in the lurch, who has no other choice; she's an old battle-ax who has to take care of herself because nobody wants her. They imply that her success is the result of necessity, that she certainly wouldn't have taken the road to the top out of conviction. But this does not answer the question "Is it power that makes you lonely, or do lonely women turn into power-hungry fighters?" Whatever the answer, women are afraid that power inevitably makes you lonely. And a woman doesn't ever want to end up as an old maid or have people think she's been jilted.

This is a hard trap to avoid. Although strong lone fighters don't have to be lonely, a committed career woman will spend less time coddling others. More likely, at the end of the workday she'd like someone to cheer *her* up. In any case, her life is certainly not without joy and friends, and she doesn't constantly think only of her job.

On the contrary, women who have well-defined career goals and do their work energetically are also doing things during their time off. They use their strength to support others, *and* their self-confidence allows them to ask friends and colleagues for help and support. They use leisure time to refuel; they enjoy vacations and have fun with friends.

Larissa has avoided the mental trap about the lonely powerful woman. She vigorously pursues her professional goal without fear of loneliness. She likes being able to make her own decisions and to assign clear responsibilities to others. It doesn't bother her when, now and then, someone on her staff becomes disgruntled, or complains, or turns her down because he or she thinks her requests are inconvenient. Larissa is into the swing of things. As the sales manager of a pharmaceutical firm, she is tough but uses tact and sensitivity to motivate her staff. She is married and the mother of two girls, seven and four years old.

People often insinuate that she is not a *real* woman. They imply she lacks all the qualities that a caring wife and good mother is supposed to have. She doesn't pack a nutritious school lunch for her children; they have to buy it in the cafeteria. And when they come home in the afternoon, although there's always someone in the house, they have to entertain themselves. She doesn't help the older one with her homework, and she doesn't even have time for that supposedly important mother-and-daughter talk when her kids come home from school. The malicious neighborhood gossips ask why she had children if she doesn't take care of them. In the evenings her husband, who is also deeply involved with his job, comes home either to an empty apartment or two wound-up children who immediately monopolize his time.

The neighbors say it's a disgrace. But is it? Larissa doesn't let the neighbors' comments bother her; she's prepared for their negative clichés. She anticipated such criticism and made sure she had the support of her friends and sympathetic colleagues. She is very concerned about the quality of relationships within her family. She is sure of herself. The time she spends playing and having fun with her kids is a pleasure for them all, and her work enriches the relationship she has with her husband. He is proud of her accomplishments.

Larissa knows that many people watch her skeptically. But her husband and children back her up. Only occasionally—when one of the children is sick, or when the older girl was afraid at the start of a new school year—is she not completely sure of herself. Whenever she has such twinges of doubt, she has a talk with her husband and with the children. For support she goes to people whose opinions she values.

Clients and colleagues, both men and women, now and then try to rattle her self-confidence. They accuse her of being insensitive to her family. That makes her wonder, but in a little while she sees her way clear again. If she's having a bad day and starts to brood, she picks up the phone and talks to her husband or a woman friend and they help to put her back on track. The support of friends is important even for strong solitary women fighters.

Although there are exceptions like Larissa, many women continue to see striving for power as taboo. Even the New Woman may at most be only a little bit ambitious. She's supposed to produce results, but she must not reach for the moon. If she does, the threat of loneliness looms before her. Only men are allowed to reach for the moon. The fear of losing your femininity lends the very word *career* a dangerous overtone—as though you'd be ready to trample on people if they got in your way. To achieve modest success must be a woman's highest goal. This unintentionally supports the mental trap about the dangers of ambition. Women don't want to and are not supposed to make careers for themselves. And so, for fear of seeming hard and cold, even an ambitious woman will deny her craving for power and her longing to have a career. She'll spend an entire evening discussing with her friends how best to camouflage her own ambitions without giving up the stereotypes of femininity and gentleness. And yet when women get left behind by their male colleagues, they feel they've been discriminated against. They go only halfheartedly after the really good jobs, held back by the worry that they will suddenly find themselves alone and lonely on the way up the ladder. They let others, usually men, get ahead, or they stay behind because of loyalty to their "nice" boss. They themselves are throwing the switch that will sidetrack their careers. When all is said and done, if they're lucky, they'll get an award for loyalty.

Many women who have good prospects for promotion or professional advancement feel such close ties or obligations to their company or their boss that they won't even consider a change. They are grateful because they are treated well; you know the old saw "A bird in the hand . . ."

Keep Your Ideas to Yourself!

All too often women stick too strictly to the rules of the game. They seldom question the handicaps, and they will accept a set of rules uncritically, even when they doubt their validity. Most of these rules serve to chain them to their roles in life.

If you always stick to the rules, you can't be creative. So you'll have little influence in changing or making things happen. Only if you devise your *own* rules—rules with which you feel comfortable—can you determine your own course. You can even decide the roles others will play for you. Only women who dare to say, "That old rule doesn't suit me; I'm going to try something new," and then act accordingly, will be able to put their good ideas to work.

Women haven't yet learned to decide for themselves how much they should let others meddle in their lives. Because they're afraid of exploiting other people, they refuse to decide what they themselves want. Even the New Woman is a "good" woman. The shackles put on her in childhood have cut deeply into her flesh. She has internalized the rules, norms, and traditions of her mother and grandmother. In her heart of hearts she tries to stick to them even if they have little application to her life and the modern view of her role. She has squeezed herself into her old role-model girdle, although she's wearing modern clothes over it.

She tells herself, "Keep your suggestions to yourself; the others know better anyway. You'll only make a fool of yourself." A woman feels guilty as soon as she finds herself wishing that she could change the rules or for once ignore them. For her, power is something that borders on blasphemy.

Take Polly, for example. She often goes bicycling with friends. She knows the surrounding area well, but she never suggests the route they should take. She's afraid the others—especially the guys—might think her a know-it-all, or worse yet, domineering. She's more familiar with the countryside than they are, but she pedals along in silence over rough back roads as the others, who think they know what they're doing, get completely lost. This happens often, and although the fun has gradually gone out of these cycling trips for her, she never speaks up.

Many women act this way. At best they may warily indicate that there are different and better solutions or directions to take, or they'll whisper it in someone's ear. In the end they're offended because nobody listened to them or paid attention to their so-called demands—which really sounded more like timid mumbling.

Reaching the Goal But Losing Anyway

What seems even worse is when women get what they want but are later accused of having run roughshod over others. The feeling of having control over others tortures women more than their own powerlessness. It is part and parcel of the fear of having abused one's power.

The New Woman has mixed feelings toward power. She's in a diabolical bind. She wants authority and is annoyed at not having any. At work she must, and wants to, accept obligations, but she doesn't have enough power to fulfill them adequately. Often she may lack the necessary budget, or she has no authority to give orders or hire people.

She is supposed to take on responsibility and wants to; she'd like to get things moving, break with traditions, and change old time-worn routines. She wants to make decisions freely and have far-reaching financial authority. But she fights only halfheartedly for her goals because she is afraid that as she gets more authority, she will be liked less. She fears that she'll appear domineering and arrogant, lose her femininity—*and all just for a little share of power.* The price seems too high.

These problems exist *between* women too. As in previous years, Susan and Rosalie jointly planned a trip. In spite of their different tastes in vacations, they wanted to go off and do something together. Susan wanted to relax; Rosalie wanted excitement. Susan suggested a lovely hotel with sauna and swimming pool not far from a large city. Surprisingly, Rosalie agreed on the spot. During their vacation, both seemed to feel as if they were on top of the world. Susan liked the combination of peace and quiet and big-city cultural activities nearby; Rosalie seemed to be in good spirits. But on the trip back she started to complain. She just couldn't stand up to Susan, she said, and felt she'd been steamrollered. Actually, she'd rather have gone to Paris—around-the-clock action there. Susan felt guilty. She was familiar with this kind of accusation; she got it from her colleagues at work, too.

So she came to me for advice and said she wanted to learn how to be less pushy. She felt like an Amazon, unfeminine and overbearing. I asked Susan to describe exactly whom she had steamrollered and when. Only after she began, almost squeamishly, to pick apart what had happened in various situations did she see how these "discussions" usually played out. She realized that *she* did not steamroller anybody, but that she made decisions that others were reluctant to make.

All the different stories she told had one thing in common: The other people generally didn't know what they wanted. But most of the time Susan did, and she said so with self-assurance. She gave the others a chance to make suggestions and was fully prepared to compromise. But they often found it a relief to go along with her proposals. Only afterwards did they begin to second-guess her. Susan's decisiveness and clarity are far from being typical female behavior, wherein directness, clarity, and single-mindedness are rarely all present at the same time. Susan was straightforward about what she thought. She was neither shy nor hesitant; she knew what she wanted, and most of the time much of what she planned actually worked out. Susan had to learn to stick with her strong qualities. She didn't want to be a "bad" girl, an egotist. But she felt like an outsider among the "good," adaptable, and compliant women who were all so terribly diplomatic. However, indecisiveness has nothing to do with diplomacy. Diplomacy is the art of negotiating. And negotiating skills produce results from which *all* parties benefit.

Power Means Exploitation

Erica, an experienced businesswoman, explained to me that she pays her employees well and that in return she expects good work. She arrived at this attitude after long soul-searching. She actually apologized for expecting commensurate work for the salaries she pays, describing in detail how she has to economize. As the owner of the firm, she makes a great effort not to misuse her power. She is almost obsessed with fear that she might be exploiting others. She works harder than she should because she doesn't want to ask too much of her employees. On the other hand, she can't afford well-paid temporary help, and she doesn't want to hire "poorly paid" temps; that would really be exploitation. Nor does she want to demand that her permanent workers put in overtime; that would be exploitation too. Nevertheless, she has never tried to find out whether her employees would be prepared to work overtime, and she hasn't asked anyone whether they think the money she *can* pay for temporary help is adequate.

The worry about exploiting people is also behind her hesitant attempts to get someone to help with the housework. She rarely asks her children or her work-stressed husband to give her a hand. The game some women play—tidying up before the cleaning woman comes—is a good example of this attitude.

Power Spoils People

Many prejudices flit through a woman's mind when she thinks of the power she might one day possess. All are triggered by fear.

Perhaps the most radical is her fear of selling her soul. She doesn't say it in so many words, but she believes power is a pact with the devil that makes you ruthless so that you relish demeaning a victim. "I couldn't tell others what to do, oh no!" Instantly there's a negative association of ideas: "It would be like assaulting someone."

A woman who exercises power is "bad." But believing that is the worst sort of emotional trap. It strikes especially deep and is seldom clearly expressed. Someone who makes a pact with the devil doesn't shrink from deception and trickery. "Good" girls can have only the barest inkling of what such a woman is capable of. And when one of their female colleagues is promoted, they exchange knowing glances, insinuating that she got her promotion by going to bed with the boss, or that her well-to-do father paid somebody off.

Don't Take on Responsibility

Whenever something goes wrong, women accept the responsibility, even if they are only marginally involved. Yet at the outset they refuse to take on important assignments because they're afraid of the responsibility. They'd rather forgo having any influence on the outcome, even though later on, if something goes wrong, they'll probably take the blame.

Exercising power means inducing others to do something even if they feel lukewarm about it or really don't want to do it. This is hard for women. For one thing, they don't want to force others to do something, and for another, they feel responsible for seeing that everything goes off perfectly. They are afraid that if people feel pressured, they will turn in poor work. And often they don't even try to find out whether a person would like to take on a particular job. They don't realize that they themselves don't always do things enthusiastically, and that they often struggle to finish a task. Yet in spite of that, they do good work. Others can, too.

A woman will demand achievements, perfection, dependability, and perseverance of herself even when she's not in the mood. Yet she doesn't expect others to have the willpower to do the same. She understands their laziness. Although she may complain and grumble about her ineffectual husband and her lackadaisical co-workers, she makes no firm demands on them.

Bosses have to give orders. This again is a handicap for women who think everyone should be able to see what needs to be done and pitch in. They don't like to direct the work because they don't want to be in charge, to order people around. Women are seldom ready to make someone change his behavior by using the "authority of their office." The more they feel they've pushed someone into something, the more responsible they feel for any errors he makes. Yet they rarely accept credit for the successes. They leave the laurels to others. "Good" girls shoulder all the burdens. They don't want to be in charge, and they confuse *authoritarian* with *authority*. But only someone with authority can get things done and exert some influence.

Power and authority are closely allied. You have authority because of your intellectual ability or practical competence, or you possess a natural authority that is inherent. This is the sort of authority that stems from a talent for interpersonal relationships and charisma; other people can sense it, and they respect it. Whoever exercises power on the basis of this natural authority is able to lead people and set things in motion.

Big Shots Bite

In addition, women have to learn to make their influence felt at the top. You can't have much faith in a department manager who promises an employee reporting to her that she may attend a seminar and then doesn't keep her promise because she couldn't stand up to *her* boss. Women believe they are at the mercy of their superiors. They're afraid that they'll lose their jobs if they get cheeky.

Sally is assistant to the manager of a retail chain. She wanted to take a half year of unpaid leave for a long-planned trip to South America. She was sure that one of her co-workers could substitute for her without any difficulty. The co-worker was ready to take on Sally's responsibilities and looked forward to the challenge; she saw it as a chance to prove herself and to ask for a comparable position in the future. Now Sally had to persuade her boss. She marshaled a whole series of arguments to show that her absence would not cause him any problems. That was important, for it wasn't enough just to convince her substitute; she had to make her influence felt at the top too. She knew that her boss didn't really want to let her go, so she took his objections seriously and shot them down, one by one. Sally knew that her boss thought she was competent, and she was sure of herself in making this request for a leave.

It was up to her. She had to use her persuasiveness to convince the people who were her superiors.

Is It Okay to Take Advantage of Connections?

Women think that it's improper and unethical to use connections to get ahead. They are afraid people will say they got a certain job only because so-and-so put in a good word for them, and this keeps them from exchanging views and establishing relationships of mutual trust with those in higher positions. They're afraid that gossips will say they intrigued or slept their way up the ladder. This fear keeps them from contacting people who have inside information. Women don't want special treatment, and using connections smacks of that. But having good connections to many colleagues is a prerequisite for getting at information that is important to effectively and successfully carry out an assignment. You cannot perform your work effectively if you are cut off from such information because you are boring and not popular or because you make yourself inconspicuous. Only if you have good connections to both your co-workers and your superiors can you have solid power.

Cultivating good connections does *not* mean doing the work of others; it means recognizing their interests and integrating them wherever possible.

Women Pull the Strings Behind the Scenes

Yes, there they are, behind the scenes, all right, but they don't have the power!

Many women are told they are the real string-pullers; that *they* are the ones who actually make the important decisions, who push their husbands into good jobs; and that they are more interested in their man's success than he is. That it's Elizabeth, not Bob, and Nancy, not Ronald, who are the real go-getters; and it isn't Mr. Jones who wears the pants, but Mrs. Jones. With a knowing smile, women wink at each other in agreement. They'd like to believe that they are influencing far-reaching developments this way.

Nobody knows how much influence a woman who stays in the background really has. That she has any at all is pure speculation; it's a claim that flatters her, praises her modesty . . . and squelches her into silence. If it really were so, then why the modesty? What keeps women from reaping the glory if they really are the ones who sowed the seed?

What makes women pull the strings behind the scenes? The explanation offered is that they supposedly fear both success and failure. Different explanations have been tailored to fit the situation. These may be interesting models to explain the workings of a woman's mind, but they're not much help in solving the problem of what women can do to put themselves in the limelight. How can they, in good conscience, gradually exercise the rights they have been promised? How can a woman learn to put up with a husband who is ashamed because he earns less than she? How can she concentrate on her job when she's feeling guilty because her fourteen-year-old daughter has problems at school? What can she do about feeling so damn guilty when her husband has to warm up TV dinners in the microwave?

What stops women isn't fear of success; it's feelings of guilt, a bad conscience, and dismay at not having been "good"—not to mention the external hurdles that are placed in their path. Unfortunately, mothers still pass these models along to their daughters. A mother who promises her child, "I'll talk with Daddy about it," and who, at night when she's alone with her husband, wheedles and charms him into granting their daughter this or that, is not really asserting herself. She doesn't take a stand openly, not even in front of her child. She thinks that parents should always be solidly united, of one opinion, the father's, of course. By her example, she is teaching her child that it is better to be manipulative than to act candidly. In contrast, the real power behind the throne is not a wheedling and flattering manipulator, but rather a competent adviser who benefits from her status.

A woman often gives her husband a push because she wants him to get an important job and earn good money. But the supposed benefit from this—to have a secure and worry-free life—backfires. She makes herself dependent and hides her abilities. Ultimately she won't even be able to provide for herself. Women often make themselves invisible. That's hardly the way to become the power behind the throne.

Must One Struggle Constantly to Retain Power?

Women think that holding on to power is stressful business. Actually the opposite is true: When you use power effectively, it leads to more power.

Women who, after a long inner struggle, decide that power is no longer taboo and use their power with sensitivity soon realize that once one has some power, it is easy to get more.

A female boss who gives her employees clearly defined assignments and supervises them to see that they are carried out, who gives them enough leeway without allowing them to waste time, is using her power sensibly. Her staff will stand behind her if she supports their requests to take training courses, implements raises, allows for appropriate overtime compensation, clearly delegates responsibility, and from time to time gives them more interesting work to do. She will then be able to do her job and prove that she can lead. Her success will be attributed to her know-how, and she'll get more demanding jobs in the future. It's the start of a positive success spiral.

"Good" Girls Don't Compete

It is often particularly difficult for a woman to delegate. She's afraid she'll make herself superfluous. It starts with unpleasant jobs she doesn't want to impose on others and ends with important assignments she's afraid to pass along because she's worried about competition. Fear of competition from her own staff leads her to delegate only unimportant tasks to them. In extreme cases she even does some routine work herself in order to make herself indispensable and to avoid nurturing a potential competitor in the office. In this way she's wasting energy she could be using for jobs that are really important to her career. She fritters herself away on incidentals and discourages the people working for her.

She's cutting off her nose to spite her face by not allowing the training of a possible successor. If and when she is offered a promotion, there'll be no one ready to take her place. And without a competent successor in the wings, her own promotion becomes less likely.

The flip side of power rears its head when a "powerful" woman feels that she's working round the clock and everybody else is resting at her expense. She feels like a high-level servant. She can't trust anyone or delegate work with a clear conscience. Added to that are the everyday demands made of a senior manager. At that point she might wish for a knight in shining armor to rescue her and to tenderly carry her up the career ladder.

Few women are aware of it, but there comes a time when they're taking on too much. The mental trap that it's best to do everything yourself so that nobody else can see the cards you hold has women working around the clock until they're exhausted. So they have no real power and don't make use of opportunities to become executives.

What's in a Title?

Women are often very casual about their names. They readily give them up when they get married, even today when one can use either the husband's or the wife's last name, or both. Along with their names many women also give up their identity. They only repeat what their husbands say; they hide behind his viewpoint, his profession, his money. They put no value on their personal image, they are merely "so-and-so's wife."

Even a woman who has overcome such obstacles and is a professional in her own right often quotes the views of her husband. She considers the titles she's achieved as unimportant and thinks that what she accomplishes at work isn't very interesting. She certainly doesn't want special attention. When they ask her what to put on the nameplate that will hang on her office door, she deliberately waives the title in front of her name. Even though she's offended when people think she's just a typist, she still doesn't use her title. She wants to make it by virtue of her abilities, she says, not on the basis of "labels." Others are supposed to recognize her ability, but she doesn't want to call it to their attention.

Sibyl has two impressive doctorate degrees and a euphonious name: Sibyl Maria Markham-Smith, Ph.D., LL.D., J.D. The sign on her office door says: S. SMITH. Even her first name sounds too exotic to her.

Titles are important. They identify a person as someone who has achieved a certain status and has certain qualifications. Titles are especially important for women because people are often skeptical about their abilities and competence. Even when women do the same jobs or take on the same assignments as men, they frequently aren't given the title that goes with the job. Titles are only reluctantly awarded to women.

Like power, titles often have a negative connotation for women. On the whole, they modestly do without titles; they don't strive for them or demand them; they feel they "don't need" them. By not using titles, they are doing without an effective door opener, a key to power, influence, and recognition. A title indicates authority. Someone with a title doesn't have to try so hard to convince others. Men create titles shamelessly; they call themselves "product engineer," "sales manager," or describe themselves as "executives." On the other hand, when you address a woman by her title, she'll frequently say, "Oh, you can skip the 'Doctor.' " That's too bad. A title is proof of their qualifications; it inspires confidence and gives them an advantage over competitors. Often they've gone to great lengths to get a certificate or degree, but then they don't want to "put on airs" by using it.

When Lizzie introduced herself to a group of professional women, she immediately apologized for not having an advanced college degree. They all assured her that it didn't matter. One of the women got up and *confessed* she didn't have an academic degree either. It would seem that for those who don't have one, an academic title really matters. So is this modesty about titles some sort of reverse snobbism? Odd, isn't it, that a woman doesn't mention her title, she simply has one. Some women with advanced degrees have an explanation: They don't use their titles at conferences or at meetings where there are men who don't have doctorates. They want to spare their male colleagues the "embarrassment."

Often at conferences attended by assistants and executive secretaries, there are women who are in charge of departments of five or more employees. But they don't introduce themselves as department heads or project managers, the way their male colleagues undoubtedly would. Modestly they remain *Administrative Assistant to the Manager,* or they call themselves "my boss's right hand" as though they weren't independent agents, but merely something with parts that can be amputated and made available to other people. A male *assistant,* however, is an aspirant to his boss's job. The female assistant is just a glorified secretary; if she's lucky, she'll move up with her boss.

Risks Must Be Avoided

Women tend to consider the exercise of power as risky. That wouldn't be the end of the world if they would only see that risk takers can also *win.* But if you talk to women about risks, it soon turns out that they always equate risk taking with the danger of losing.

Particularly in the business world, hesitation is almost always penalized with economic drawbacks and losses. Every firm has one or more aggressive competitor. In this sort of climate only a courageous company policy can succeed in the long run. Only a management that is ready to take risks will be successful. Halfhearted decision making, a wait-and-see attitude, and maneuvering almost inevitably lead to failure. However, women equate courage with recklessness and foolhardiness.

Even when it comes to investing their own money, women go for the sure thing. As a rule they favor the safest type of investment, even if they get only small returns. They prize security and dismiss chances for bigger profits. In addition, women are afraid that they don't understand enough about business matters, so they usually choose popular, fixed-interest securities suggested by their bank. This inclination to avoid risks applies to almost all areas. Because they are afraid of making a wrong decision, women would rather play it safe. A woman may take a gamble by going to a new vacation spot, but at work she's loyal to her employer. Women change employers less frequently than men—even when the chance for a better job beckons. This applies even to women in management positions.

Career advisers emphasize how important it is for your future to prove yourself in various jobs. They consider it essential for someone who wants to reach a managerial position to switch jobs every three to five years. But women hesitate. The "good girls" still believe that loyalty pays off in the end.

Only a few dare to take a leap into the unknown, and usually only when they are supported or pushed by others.

Power Makes You Unpopular

There's a deep-seated fear that the more influence and power you have, the less you will be liked by those around you.

Regina and Clarissa are good friends, even though Regina is Clarissa's boss. In the middle of Clarissa's scheduled vacation, at a time when most of the staff were also away, two employees became ill. Regina felt bad: What a time to have to call Clarissa and ask her to interrupt her vacation; only a week earlier a beaming Clarissa had told her all the things she planned to do with her son during this vacation.

Regina, who was determined to fill the shoes of the department manager while he was away, knew that there'd be a row with Clarissa if she asked her to come in to help out. And the "glory" of being a manager just wasn't worth that. She'd rather work day and night herself. And even though she knew that she couldn't get the work done without Clarissa, she decided, for the time being, not to call her. She could understand why Clarissa wanted to spend her vacation with her son. And she was afraid to lose a friend if she made use of her temporary power. She'd rather work till late at night and over the weekend.

When Regina finally realized that she couldn't get the job done on time, it was too late—Clarissa and her son had left town.

Regina missed deadlines. She felt miserable and told herself, "I should have known that I'm not suited for a job like this." Her fear of being disliked had kept her from acting rationally.

Regina was not able to use her power as temporary manager to make the department function smoothly. She didn't understand that as boss, it was her job to assign her staff to tasks so that the operation would run efficiently, without complications and delays. She had valued her friendship with Clarissa more highly than the demands of the office.

That Regina understood and respected Clarissa's vacation plans is certainly laudable. But understanding must not become a trap. Regina should have called Clarissa back to work.

Women often find it difficult to order others to do things that they themselves would find unpleasant or burdensome. For them, understanding others means letting them do as they like.

It is hard for women to get other people to accept and cope with uncomfortable situations because as little girls, they learned to make life as comfortable as possible for others.

Regina is a typical example of how women want to smooth unpleasant or inconvenient things out of the way for other people. She doesn't even ask her cleaning woman to do any disagreeable tasks around the house.

Millie is a department manager. She permits her employees to decide when they want to take their vacations and then schedules her own vacation accordingly. She works overtime so that her staff can go home on time. She deals with grumpy customers so her employees won't have to. During lunch hour she answers the telephones. She does all this because she is solicitous and concerned for her employees and because she wants them to like her.

It's nice when you get along well with the people with whom you spend most of the day. Yet on the job it is important to *work* well together. You don't have to like one another all that much.

Of course, it would be totally wrong to eliminate all warm and friendly relationships at work. A pleasant atmosphere is important. And it is also important to maintain good contacts. But it is wrong to make sacrifices and expect that others will love you for it.

A woman can use power effectively only when she is respected by her co-workers. To do her job well, she has to fit into the firm's social fabric.

To use your own position meaningfully you need the recognition and respect of your staff. Along with that goes a certain degree of popularity, not because you are nice, meek, and servile, but because you've earned it by being dependable and fair—through level-headed detachment and mutual respect.

Women must establish personal contacts and keep up connections. In that way they can plug into an effective information network and can assure themselves of the support of those above *and* below them. Of course, the rumor mills begin to grind as soon as a woman takes up even a semiprivate relationship with a male employee or a superior. In such a case it is important to be straightforward and unambiguous. Don't make a secret of any personal relationship; don't have two-tier relationships—if you're on an informal basis with someone in private, then continue that at work. Enter into an intimate or flirting relationship only if and when you really want to. You'll rarely gain any professional benefits from it. Raising a colleague's hopes, consciously or unconsciously, will almost always boomerang.

Problems also frequently crop up in friendships between women who have jobs on different levels within the company hierarchy.

You can't maintain the total commitment in a friendship that says, "I'll always be there for you. You'll always come first with me," no matter how good your intentions.

You *can* keep up a good friendship that is limited to a narrower aspect of your life, e.g., "I like playing tennis with you. I like listening to your opinions. I enjoy your company." But here's a warning: At work be careful about becoming pals for the wrong reasons.

"Whoever Exalts Himself Will Be Humbled"

Even the Bible teaches false modesty.

Women are often afraid: If I rise above my female co-workers, they won't like me any more and they'll work against me.

Shirley had been office manager for several months, in charge of fifteen workers. One day she had a splendid idea: She would organize a monthly supper get-together for the secretaries in her office. So she rented a room in a restaurant and ordered a modest meal for her staff. It would give them a chance to talk about all kinds of things.

The secretaries were enthusiastic about the idea. Shirley was on good terms with these women, and she hoped to gain their trust and support. She had the impression that they all accepted and respected her. Now, she thought, she would really be one of them.

The monthly suppers were well attended. Shirley was pleased.

But the other day, on the way to the restaurant, she felt uncomfortable. At the last meeting, as she approached the dining room, she had heard a lively babble of happy voices, but as soon as she walked in, the jolly mood seemed to change and an embarrassed silence took its place. Smiling bravely, she said, "Don't let me interrupt you." But somehow the bubble had burst. Shirley was disappointed. Why should her presence disturb these women? After all, the whole thing had been her idea, and she thought that her staff really liked her.

Shirley felt rejected, even betrayed. She suspected the women were bad-mouthing her behind her back. They would offer her friendly smiles, but in reality they rejected her. She had hoped to be boss and friend at the same time. Now it pained her to see that her staff apparently considered her the authority in charge. And yet she felt as though she was their friend, a buffer between them and those in the front office, a protective shield. She wanted to be an equal among equals.

Her wish is understandable. Belonging gives you a feeling of security and closeness. But if you're an equal among equals, you can't be their superior, regardless of how genuine your own feelings of solidarity may be. No matter how sincere Shirley's feelings toward her staff were, she was the person in charge. And occasionally her job included firing people who did not work out. Shirley can become a sympathetic and respected boss, but she can't also be her employees' friend. She will have to look for friends among those who have positions on the same level as hers. That has nothing to do with arrogance, it's simply inevitable. Because of her role as a supervisor, she cannot "belong" to the circle of her employees, even though she may wish to. Her position places her a rung above her staff. The monthly meetings are a good idea, but Shirley has to stay in the background if she wants her "team" to enjoy these get-togethers. Now and then she can look in on the sessions, but very gingerly. Trying to be pals with "the wrong people" can be just as damaging as keeping an exaggerated distance.

Most people know that in everyday life, as soon as a man or a woman becomes differentiated from other members of a group who were their former equals, whether through education, work status, motherhood, wealth, or poverty, he or she quickly loses contact with the "old friends." This applies to almost everyone. Of course, there are exceptions. But generally people feel close to and comfortable with those with whom they have a great deal in common.

Women Also Have to Be Bosses

Karen runs a large firm that deals in automotive equipment. Five years ago, after she completed her studies in mechanical engineering, she took charge of the business, which had been run by her father. She represents the third generation of family ownership, and she has known several of the older employees since her childhood. She feels comfortable working there. She used to help out now and then and knows all the people who work there, not only their career ambitions, but most of their worries, crises, and joys. She felt it was natural—no, it was her duty—to be concerned for these people. So she became excessively considerate of her employees' problems.

Karen's personal assistant had been working for the company for fifteen years as a secretary. Karen knew that the woman was supporting her family with her earnings. She had two adolescent kids and an alcoholic husband who only sporadically earned any money. Family relations were difficult and stressful, and Karen often talked things over with her assistant, supporting her with help and advice. She allowed her to take pay advances and was often on the phone with her late into the night. Karen would help when her assistant's husband had to go back into the clinic and when there was trouble with the children.

Karen felt an obligation to help. This woman's fate was in her hands, and yet she felt she must not exploit her power as head of the firm. Anyway, it made Karen uncomfortable that so many people depended on her. The least she could do was to show that she would do whatever she could for them.

Her assistant wasn't the only person Karen helped. She had found someone to baby-sit for the child of a single woman who worked for her, and she had arranged for the elderly father of another of her employees to be admitted to a nursing home. She raised no objection when two of her employees who were attending night school to get their high school degrees left fifteen minutes early every afternoon.

The other aspect of her maternal benevolence was that Karen herself worked till late at night. She could understand why her employees wanted to leave at 4:45 P.M. But she had to be available to clients, at least by telephone, until 6:00 P.M. It would have been a lot better for the business if there had been a small sales staff available between 4:45 and 6:00. But she couldn't afford that expense, and she didn't dare ask some of her employees to take a long lunch hour in exchange for working later. And so she was forced to hire temporary help to answer the telephones till closing time. In the summer the operation almost broke down because Karen had allowed too many employees to take their vacations at the same time.

She was always sympathetic. Rarely was she able to give priority to her own interests and those of the firm. People, she felt, came first, and other people mattered more than she did. This attitude came on top of Karen's fear of exploiting her power. Her grandfather had coined the company motto: "He who has power also has responsibility." But Karen didn't notice the "also"; she thought she had only the responsibility. She became a victim of her idealism, completely losing sight of her own and the firm's interests. She frittered away her energies and time in caring and mothering her employees. After four years she had to sell the company.

Chapter 4

Various Strategies

·

Discover Your Worth

Women often have a hard time recognizing their own merits. Even when they think they have special qualifications and skills, they find it difficult to see that this makes them valuable. Here are a number of things you can do to assure yourself of your own worth.

Speak to people who are on your side. Get them to tell you what they especially value about you, both personally and professionally.

List important deals and decisions you've made for which you alone were responsible.

If you were able to persuade someone to do something, try to understand just how you did it.

Stress your know-how and emphasize your skills.

If you live by yourself or are contemplating a separation from your husband or partner, and you feel that you don't have a good handle on your finances, take to heart the following bit of advice: **Get a clear picture of your income and your expenses. Set up a budget. It will help you to get along better on your own income.**

Many women think they need a man to guarantee their economic security, to confirm their attractiveness, to be taken seriously, to avoid being considered a competitor by other women, and last but not least, to keep from being called an old maid.

So they continue in relationships they don't really want anymore. They worry about how they can hold on to their husbands, making all sorts of sacrifices instead of developing strategies to solve problems that might arise if they found themselves *without* a husband.

You have to clarify to yourself the motives that caused you to make certain decisions, and to work out solutions that target these motives directly.

If you're afraid of being considered an old maid, ask yourself: What is it about this label that affects me so negatively? You can then develop an attitude that will effectively counteract the image.

Recognize Your Achievements

Identifying your accomplishments is essential if you want to shake off the Cinderella role. And it will work for you if you do a little self-assessment:

⚠

For at least two days a week, jot down, in detail, all the things you did really well during that time.

Make sure that you describe your achievements in positive terms: My idea for finishing the attic is really fabulous. I'm very good at making my lectures interesting and colorful. I like the way I decorated my apartment. I prepared my students very well for their examination. I'm good at making striking flower arrangements. I can persuade people and bring them around

to my point of view. I've got musical talent and sing quite well.

If you feel like it, go a step further and write a paragraph in praise of yourself. Imagine that you have to convince another person that you're qualified for, let's say, getting your dream job. At first it's often difficult to recognize and acknowledge your own achievements. Women have been taught to be modest. So have men, but they rarely stick to this precept. Women feel they are boasting, making a fuss, or showing off as soon as they begin to describe their accomplishments objectively. They must learn to assess these achievements realistically.

Pay Attention to Your Needs

One way to avoid mental traps is to define your own needs.

First, imagine you are completely independent and can freely plan what to do with your time. Given your present situation, what would you most like to do?

Perhaps this assignment sounds absurd because right now you don't live by yourself and you have to go to work, and so everything is different. Nevertheless, try to think of what you would do if . . . Stick to the idea that you are deciding this only for yourself, and then map out all the different possibilities in detail. Only after you know exactly what you want to do, ask yourself whether you would like someone to join you, and if so, who it would be.

Next, tell that particular person or persons how you see things and what you are planning to do, and find out if and how far they are prepared to go along with you.

Try to determine just how important your goal is to you. Ask yourself: Am I ready to go it alone? What could make me compromise? On what issues am I ready to compromise? Where do I draw the line? How useful are other people to me? What do they get out of supporting me or holding me back?

Pass Tasks Along to Others

This is especially hard to do when the work is a cinch for you. At first glance it seems senseless to watch another person struggling to accomplish something you could do with one arm tied behind your back. But in the long run it's very useful. You don't have to do things that others can do as well. They'll get it done, and you'll be relieved of some of the burden. Furthermore, this principle is valid not only at work. For example:

Kim paid an acquaintance to type her doctoral thesis. As a result, she had time to prepare for the orals. And she earned more money from a temporary job than the typing had cost her.

Inez and another mother in the neighborhood take turns every other week picking their children up from kindergarten. So every second week Inez can work later at the office putting in more hours. This is a real help for a woman who is raising her child by herself.

Jessica is a freelance tax adviser. She has hired an office assistant even though, after half a year on her own, she isn't making much money. But the assistant takes care of all the tedious and time-consuming tasks that, if she had to do them, would leave Jessica less time for updating her files, keeping up with tax law interpretations, and meeting with clients.

The same principle also applies to a woman working for someone else. For her, it's even more important to avoid having to do all the time-consuming, routine jobs that are not really rewarded anywhere. You get recognition for new ideas, well-planned improvements, and surefire suggestions. But thinking things through and making sure they'll work out requires time. And you can only free up such time by delegating routine tasks.

Mildred is the head of the personnel department of a large mail-order house. Whenever she needs files, she goes to the archives and gets them herself; she does it on principle. At first glance, her reasoning makes sense: She worked her way up in the firm and knows her way around. She can find the files faster than her secretary. Besides, the sooner she's found the documents, the sooner she'll be able to get her work done. She'd feel a little arrogant asking her secretary to search for a file when she herself knows exactly where it is.

Most women find it difficult to delegate. Often they're afraid of making themselves superfluous. The more complex the task to be delegated, the greater their fear. With this handicap they spoil their chances for promotion. Afraid of training a future competitor, they get bogged down with all the tedious details of their job. This becomes a brake on their climb up the professional ladder.

Here are a few guidelines for finding out when to delegate. Jot down five things you've wanted to do for a long time that are important for your work. For example, to read a specialized book or article, or to register for a computer course. Take any day of the week and list all the things you usually do yourself but that someone else could do equally well. Write down the names of people who could take on some of these tasks and assign them—for now, only on paper.

On a day when you're in a good mood, ask one of the people on your list to take on a certain job. As you do this, pay special attention to your inhibiting thoughts. Here are a few examples of mental traps you might encounter:

I hope nothing goes wrong. After all, she doesn't have any experience with that.

I ought to do this myself; I could do it faster.

Actually that's part of *my* job.

She will think I'm bossy if I give her assignments.

She will surely think I'm overbearing if I don't do it myself.

If I let others do my work for me, I shouldn't be surprised if the boss gets the idea that he doesn't need me anymore.

I ought to do that myself, then it will be done right.

I can't expect anyone else to do that, the job is too . . .

If I put that on her desk, she'll think me presumptuous.

Thoughts like these keep women from heading straight for their goal. You can escape these mental traps by identifying them and disarming them. In mental training sessions these mental traps are called *negative thinking.* Why not change over to new *positive thinking?* It's quite simple: Whenever you hit a mental trap, confront your negative thinking with the following positive guidelines:

⚠

I'll stay calm even if my staff don't approach the job as I expect them to. I'll use the time I've gained by delegating jobs to work on my own things. I will spend the time meaningfully, doing important tasks that require full concentration.

Even if the other employees disapprove, I'll stay cool and stick to my assignment, which will better focus my resources. My employees don't have to love me.

You have to draw the line before you burn out. Women who aspire to do exciting, promising work have to realize there are only twenty-four hours in each day. Moreover, pretty soon they'll have to face the fact that they have only a limited amount of energy. Therefore, if you take on a new assignment, you have to give up others. And the first one to go, of course, has to be the job that's most unpleasant for you, that you'd most like to get rid of. Your immediate impulse may be to delegate a pleasant task, but—you've guessed it—that would be a mental trap.

Once you accept the fact that it's necessary to delegate the unpleasant work, your career path will get easier.

Make a list of all your tasks and prioritize them—

- *From:* I want to get rid of this one as soon as possible (it doesn't contribute to my professional advancement, it's monotonous or boring). *To:* I want to do that one myself, no matter what (the job has good prospects/it's fun).
- Make a list of the qualifications needed for the tasks you want to get rid of. Then match these qualifications with people who you think will do the tasks well.

Various Strategies

While you're making the assignments, listen with your inner ear. What are the "ifs" and "buts" that are skulking around in your head? Take the time to examine each objection and discover your inner hurdles.

Learn to Say NO!

Saying "no" with confidence is the first step on the way from being a "good girl" to being a "bad girl"—being able to refuse some demands, including reasonable ones, without feeling guilty and without letting it get you down. You must even be able to say "no" to a close girlfriend, otherwise the transformation will be only superficial.

After many weeks of hard work, Eve was looking forward to a lazy Sunday at home. Just then Stacy called to ask her to baby-sit for her four-year-old twins. Stacy obviously had an important reason for asking. Her friend of many years and the father of her children wanted to leave her. And Stacy was eager to have a long talk with him in a last-ditch attempt to salvage their relationship. He had bought a plane ticket, and in a few hours he'd be going to the airport and then he'd disappear for half a year if Stacy couldn't get him to live up to his obligations. Eve understood why Stacy wanted to get the twins off her hands for a couple of hours, but for the first time ever, she refused one of Stacy's requests. She didn't want to waste her precious time to assist in this constantly recurring melodramatic maneuver which was bound to fail.

Stacy was taken aback. She hadn't expected this reaction. "You're leaving me in the lurch!" she yelped.

"And you just want to get me involved in your senseless campaign," Eve said. She thought of all the endless sessions in which Stacy and her boyfriend had tried to clarify their relationship, and she got angry. At that point Stacy immediately changed her tactics and began to whimper—something she did very rarely. Eve knew that she'd soon start to cry. So she beat her to it. "Look, Stacy, I will not watch your children under any circumstances!" she said, and hung up.

For some time afterward Eve was filled with uncertainty. Should she change her mind and agree to do it after all? No, she wouldn't budge. First of all, she knew that Stacy's discussions with her boyfriend always ran into a blind alley; second, she sensed how urgently she herself needed a rest; and third, she remembered all the times she had given one-sided help and support to Stacy.

It worked. At last Eve relaxed and was able to listen to some music without feeling guilty.

⚠

This is how saying "no" works:
- **Admit to yourself that you want to say "no."**
- **Clearly visualize the situation and the person to whom you want to say "no."**
- **Be aware of the traps this person can use to keep you from saying "no"—with looks, gestures, by arousing your sympathy or asking you to be understanding, etc.**
- **Think of a key sentence that you can use to defend yourself against the other person's traps, such as: "Even if she gives me an angry look, I'll stay calm and firm," or "Even if I feel sorry for her, I'll stick to my 'no.'"**
- **You must feel determined to adhere to your "no."**
- **After sticking to your guns, look ahead to what you are going to do next.**

You can only convince others that you mean "no" if you yourself are convinced.

If you think you don't have the right to say "no" or if you tell yourself beforehand that you won't be able to carry it through, then that's exactly what will happen!

Chapter 5

The
Self-Fulfilling
Prophecy

.

What the textbooks term a self-fulfilling prophecy describes a system that human beings use to keep their "destiny" intact. For instance, even if your mind tells you that as a woman you are just as good as a man, you may have hidden doubts that this is true. Perhaps you are only *almost* as good and you have to be content with "the bird in the hand."

Obviously many decent women would rather hold on to their I-can't-do-that self-image than match their strength against that of others, to go beyond their own limits, and to enjoy their successes.

Anyone who has a negative image of herself—and that's also a prophecy—will turn it into reality.

Because of the lives they have led, many women have only modest expectations of their future, their own strength, and their professional success. All the same, it is futile to complain about having had a "bad" childhood or to mourn missed opportunities. What would make a difference is for you to become aware of your own negative thinking and replace it with positive ideas. Peter H. Ludwig performed the following experiment, illustrating the power of the imagination:*

---

*Ludwig, Peter H., *Sich selbst erfüllende Prophezeiungen im Alltagsleben* (Self-fulfilling Prophecies in Everyday Life). Stuttgart, 1991.

A subject holds one end of a string. A weight has been fastened to the other end. The subject is told (1) not to move his hand and (2) to imagine the weight moving in a certain manner. After some time the weight begins to move the way the subject imagined.

Other experiments have shown that athletes can improve their performances when they have positive expectations, and that students do better work when they respond to the positive expectations of their teachers.

Thus faith can not only move mountains, but it also influences performance, mood, and much more.

Everybody knows that if you believe in something, it will often come to pass.

Paula knows that she can influence the behavior of others through the expectations she has of them. If she thinks a new colleague is a kind man, he turns out to be just that. Merely the manner in which you greet a person, the way you treat him, can turn him into a kind, pleasant individual.

If you are about to take an examination and expect the examiner to flunk you, you may treat him in such a way that he turns unfriendly and cross.

The attitude you have toward a person will not by itself change him into a good or a bad human being, but it does affect his feelings toward you at any given time.

If you feel you got out on the wrong side of the bed, you'll grab the clothes that you always wear when you're in a bad mood; you'll put on a sulky expression, miss the bus, and get to the office feeling annoyed and irritable. Doubtless the boss will grumble about your being late.

These are situations everyone is familiar with and can understand. Sometimes it is difficult to detect the self-fulfilling prophecy at work. It reaches back to expectations that lie concealed in us all. Often it is difficult to figure out whether you are steering your fate, or a hidden expectation is setting the course.

When people think that something is happening through no fault or effort of their own, when they are afraid that they have no control over certain events, a self-fulfilling prophecy (SFP) is at work.

It is hard to know whether an attitude or the outcome of a situation is caused by SFP. You can never be one hundred percent sure how a situation would have turned out with or without SFP. It helps if you become aware of your own expectations, decipher your unconscious inner messages, and think beforehand about what expectations you might possibly have. You should also explore your expectations *after* an event has occurred. That will train you in self-awareness.

This system also works when it comes to personal performance and achievement wherein women tend to think of themselves as stupid. They expect to fail and so they have no self-confidence. If you think you are mediocre or even stupid, you're bound to have little interest in something that requires intelligence. Therefore, you will probably pay little attention to the job and you'll do poorly or just so-so. If a woman thinks she's competent, she'll be in control of a particular situation because past experience has shown that she can influence events.

Stephanie was about to ask for a raise. She was sure that her work warranted one. She and a friend rehearsed what she was going to say to her boss and ticked off all the arguments to support her request. When she approached her boss, she was so convincing that he, in addition to giving her the raise, suggested she head up one of the departments.

Iris was summoned to jury duty. She wanted to get out of it on the grounds that she was indispensable both at work and at home. As a working mother of two children, she felt that this would not be a problem. She was convinced she was right, and her conviction increased as she and her husband rehearsed the talk she would have with her boss. Without hesitation, her boss wrote a letter certifying that she was indispensable to the company. He did so even though he was a firm believer in the jury system and no one else at work had ever asked for a similar letter.

The outcome isn't always so dramatically successful. At other times Stephanie and Iris may have experienced situations influenced by learned helplessness. But they know that learned helplessness doesn't have to be a permanent character trait. It is merely something you acquired in childhood, something that can be overcome. If something goes wrong, it is only temporary. The same story can turn out happily another time, when you're having a better day.

Just as positive expectations can promote a good outcome, negative expectations can turn into a stumbling block. It may not be maliciously intended, but behind the warning "Be careful" there is always the message "I don't think you are capable of doing that." There is an English children's story by David McKee about King Rollo that illustrates this situation: King Rollo wants to climb a tree. Everybody warns him, You'll fall down and hurt yourself, You'll get your hands dirty, You'll tear your jacket. But King Rollo is stubborn and determined. In the end, he actually does fall down and has to listen to all the killjoys saying, we told you so. But Rollo had fun. That was his reward for not having paid attention to the "well-intended" warnings. Triumphantly he exclaims, I said I would climb to the top—and it was terrific!

Do warnings like the following sound familiar?

"Careful, don't fall into the water."

"Did you prepare your lecture thoroughly?"

"Don't make a fool of yourself!"

"You want to learn to ski—at your age?"

Just think of the numerous messages girls are bombarded with during their childhood and adolescence! If you visualize the role models they're supposed to follow, then the expectations women are fulfilling become quite clear. And even a woman who is conscious of all the baggage she has carried around since her childhood days is not immune to getting caught up in self-fulfilling prophecies. She thinks her abilities depend on coincidence or other people. She assumes her defeats are due to her (female) nature. Then, if people, perhaps a worried girlfriend, come along and express doubts and criticisms, they are stirring up a hornets' nest of negative expectations. They are able to arouse these feelings of insecurity in her only because she already had secret doubts. The destructive seed they sow falls on the fertile soil of the self-fulfilling prophecy.

Rebecca, an architect, wanted to take over the planning for a large construction project. Her boss was not sure he could entrust the assignment to her. His hesitation alone was enough to make Rebecca feel insecure. She did get the job, but day in and day out she got on her colleagues' nerves with questions to which she already knew the answers. Her boss became angry, criticized the way she was handling the project, and put somebody else in charge.

Vanessa, fourteen, looks very much like her aunt. In school her aunt was a real dunce in math, and so Vanessa thinks she resembles her in that, too. She expects that all her efforts in math are useless; therefore, instead of studying hard, she only does what she thinks is absolutely necessary. And so she proves to herself that she can't do math. Nobody notices that whenever Vanessa has trouble in other areas, she goes all out in math; she really studies, and she always does well and holds her head above water. Unintentionally her entire family has had a part in fulfilling the collective prophecy.

Self-fulfilling prophecies that interlock like gears can derail the happiness of an entire family. One sociologist described a married couple's ongoing quarrel. The wife complained that from time to time her husband would turn into a silent recluse. When she grumbled, things got worse. After a while he withdrew into his shell even before she began to complain. And so, expecting him to clam up and withdraw, she would start to nag. Both found their expectations confirmed.

Even if you believe you are doing everything possible to forestall negative expectations, you sometimes are stoking the very fire you want to put out. Take the following example: A teacher has found that students repeatedly mispronounce a word in a foreign language. She tries to prevent the error by describing to her students how *not* to pronounce the word. And what happens? They inevitably remember the wrong pronunciation.

A constructive version of this vicious circle occurs when optimists have positive expectations and in the end discover something good even in their failures. For example: When a teacher knows that the parents of one of his pupils are college graduates, he expects good things from their child. The child senses this positive assessment and is encouraged by it. He is motivated because he feels accepted; he is attentive, takes part in classwork, and does better than he would have without this incentive.

That also explains the image people have of themselves, whether they consider themselves intelligent or insignificant—losers, victims, or lucky winners. And just as birds of a feather flock together, the more you expect success or failure, the more you will succeed or fail.

Women who learned, as little girls, that they were worth less than others develop a self-image matching the expectations that have been drummed into them.

Moreover, self-images become fixed because people have selective memories. They remember things that confirm their beliefs, and then they think that this is reality. Things you expect are easier to perceive and are seen more clearly. Something that contradicts your ideas usually is unexpected and more quickly forgotten. Fred, for instance, is always in a bad mood. Every morning his colleagues notice that he sulks around the office. When for once he arrives in a good mood, no one notices.

We see what we're accustomed to seeing, and we notice what we expect to see.

If you can't help seeing something that doesn't fit your preconceived notions, then the *exception* proves the rule.

Learned Helplessness

Self-fulfilling prophecies don't spring up in a vacuum. Both the optimist and the pessimist learn to perceive their surroundings in a certain way, to interpret and to make predictions. Whether you believe you can change things or not depends on your past experiences. If you think you have no influence on the outcome of a situation, you feel that you're at the mercy of circumstances: "You have to take life as it is." In other words, you see life as a natural catastrophe. Someone like that has "learned" to be helpless.

Almost everyone would like to know what tomorrow, next year, or the next decade has in store. Some go to a fortune-teller who reads the future in cards or in tea leaves. You feel more secure when you know what's in store for you. This feeling of security is deceptive. You think you can foresee an event, and feel betrayed by fate when what you expected doesn't happen. On the other hand, it's somewhat grotesque if you feel bad even when a negative expectation is *not* fulfilled. The very experience of having misjudged a situation makes you feel insecure.

This loss of control, the conviction that one has no influence over the outcome of a situation, is one of the reasons so many women put up with living in such poor circumstances. They have decided not to expect any more from life. Surprisingly, they feel secure in a situation like that; they are familiar with it. They learned early on to adjust to the murkier side of life. A switch to the sunny side of success, power, influence, or simple joy brings with it the danger of defeat and loss of face. Women predict ruin for themselves on unfamiliar terrain. They know where they stand if they're dependent; they know what to expect, they can handle this miserable situation. They have created niches and survival shelters for themselves. But they are fooling themselves with these presumed coping mechanisms. Submitting in silence is no solution. Neither are threatening gestures. Women don't expect to be able to deal with difficult situations. Every change, even one for the better, is seen as an incalculable risk and therefore dangerous.

Digging Up Memories

Discover mechanisms and rituals that have become ingrained by "rummaging through your memory":

1. Find out what messages you remember from your childhood.

Talk with friends and siblings, cousins, aunts, parents, and grandparents and ask them what life was like when you were a child. Which of the things you were taught then are still part of the rules that govern your life today?

First of all, you have to recognize that certain processes are at work. You can do this by observing recurring situations and finding the common elements in them until you are convinced that "this situation can be changed."

To be aware of a process doesn't mean you want to influence it. You will only decide whether you really want to change something in step number three.

You won't make any decisions about changes until your personal behavior patterns have become clear to you.

2. Find out what expectations (including unintentional ones) determine your behavior.

The effect an expectation will have is not dependent on whether it leads consciously, intentionally, or unintentionally in a certain direction.

3. Find out what expectations you have of other people and whether you yourself are perhaps fulfilling expectations other people have of you.

The better you know the "baggage" you're carrying around from your childhood, the simpler it is to recognize your own and other people's hidden expectations. That also applies to expectations that are based on your own experiences. In the process you must remember that *any* remark that unintentionally steers a person's expectation in a certain direction might already be initiating a self-fulfilling prophecy. Even the way a person looks may trigger a particular expectation. You may take an immediate liking to somebody, even though you don't know her—but she looks like a good friend from the past. And so, expecting that this person will be just as pleasant, you greet her with a cordial hello and immediately discover her likable side.

The Self-Fulfilling Prophecy

Certain expectations are frequently connected with personal appearance. For instance, people who wear glasses are usually considered intelligent, hardworking, but lacking in humor. Likewise, blondes are thought of as sexy. If someone is dressed well, you assume she is intelligent. If you take an immediate liking to a person, you also assume that she is smart. If that person resembles someone you know, then you ascribe to her the same characteristics. It will be hard to correct your preconceived notions; most of the time one stubbornly sticks to these first impressions.

That's How I Am—I Can't Change

Everybody has a fairly rigid view of his own abilities and personality. This self-concept starts and grows out of childhood experiences and is stabilized as one gets older. Later, people behave largely in accordance with this self-concept. From their experiences they filter out whatever fits the image they have of themselves. The self-fulfilling prophecy is reinforced.

In this way, a woman who feels that she isn't brave enough to go off on vacation by herself may never risk taking a trip alone.

If you think you're equipped with poor visual mapping skills, it will dampen your enthusiasm for studying interior design. If you're convinced that you lack coordination, any desire to learn to ski will be nipped in the bud. Thinking you're afraid to do something will curb your enthusiasm for it. The idea that you are boring will thwart all of your attempts to approach others. If you think poorly of yourself, you won't notice that other people accept you, or you'll interpret their acceptance in such a way that it confirms your negative self-image.

Can you imagine going on a weekend hike or a long trip by yourself? Can you imagine going to a ski exercise class? Can you imagine registering for a beginner's course in ballroom dancing?

Helen is a salesperson in a boutique. Unexpectedly one Saturday she finds she is the only one working in the store. Somehow she gets through the day, and her boss praises her. Later, Helen's comment is: "Obviously she didn't think I could do it. That wasn't praise; she was only relieved that I didn't foul up."

Someone lacking self-confidence is going to credit most of her achievements to external circumstances. Irene had sketched a new layout for her kitchen. The interior designer at the Kitchen Studio was enthusiastic when he saw it. But Irene brushed it off, saying, "That was nothing special; the catalogs all show you how to do it. And I learned how to draw from my father."

Whoever credits her successes to external causes and blames all her failures on herself is creating a negative self-image. Even if her success is due to intensive study or hard work, she won't use it to boost her image. She'll keep looking for another explanation until the negative expectation is confirmed. This has one apparent advantage: You yourself can't change much anymore, and you don't have to try hard to improve. It wouldn't work anyway. You accept failures as unavoidable, and that protects you from disappointments.

Even after something has succeeded and you realize that you were wrong in your negative self-assessment, your expectations don't change. I call this "conservation of expectations." Expectations, like prejudices, are enormously stable and devilishly resistant to change. It is hard to convince a person of her ability once she thinks she is incompetent.

This resistance to change has serious consequences for women, who are programmed to be helpless from early childhood on. The feeling of having no control over events that affect you, coupled with the expectation that these events are unchangeable, forces women into social dependence. They need someone to tell them, "That's okay. You did that well. You are good." When all is said and done, however, they frequently don't believe these assurances.

Rarely do women see themselves as creating the situations they find themselves in, and they are therefore seldom ready to consciously take responsibility for themselves and their future. They believe too many things are determined by fate. Deep down they are convinced they are helpless, no matter how assertively they act or how well they manage. At best they consider themselves good at bluffing. They only playact the role of a strong woman.

But a woman can learn effective coping strategies. To do so she must find new models to understand success and failure. It is important for her to constantly remind herself, "There is a solution, and I can find it even if I break norms and violate the rules." That is the best route to self-assertion.

The prescription for preventing helplessness is simple: Exercise control at the earliest possible time in your life. In the learned-helplessness theory, control means being able to influence the outcome of a situation. For instance, if I have the nerve to climb up this wall, I can reach the cherries in the tree. If I study hard, I will do better. If I go to bed late, I'll be tired the next day. Other people will only know what I want if I make demands.

You can't revise your childhood. Only the future is in your hands.

Either you think of your life as fixed and unchangeable, or you decide to do something—to change the things you don't like.

Helplessness is learned, and can therefore be *unlearned.* You can do this by following a program that allows you to experience, step by step, that specific Behavior A will have specific Consequence B.

A woman afraid to leave the house because she thinks something bad will happen to her has to overcome her fear in gradual increments, one step at a time. Little by little she will see that nothing bad is happening. First she has to *imagine* herself going out; next she actually takes the first steps outside her door in the company of another person; then, amid familiar surroundings, she goes out by herself.

The hardest part of this assignment is to get yourself to act, since helpless people have learned to behave passively. Smiling is frequently a sign of passivity. Insecure and modest people will smile in embarrassment and do nothing. Behind their smiles they feel defeated. By and large they consider themselves unable to exert any control. They hope that if they just smile and stay quiet, the cup, whatever its contents, will "pass from them."

It is to some degree a relief to be passive. For the last two years a woman in assertiveness training has been avoiding trying to get a specialist's job. She describes her present job as follows: "I don't have to worry whether I'll be able to do everything well or whether I am as good as my colleagues. I don't have to do anything except sit at my desk and do the filing."

The consequences of such passivity are serious. In an experiment, subjects were given some texts to proofread.* They were exposed to loud noise while they were working. Those who *believed* that they could not turn off or lower the noise, who assumed they had to put up with it, did worse than those who assumed that they could get away from the noise although they had been advised not to turn it off. Both groups were exposed to the same level of noise.

The subjects who were convinced that they could control the noise, even though they were "mistaken," did better with the assignment.

Other investigations demonstrated that people who cannot control certain situations will transfer this experience to other situations. That is, they do not expect to be able to exert any influence over later events either, and thus they behave passively.

Two researchers presented students with a set of problems, some solvable, some not.** For example, two cards were held up in front of a subject, one white and one black. Behind one of the cards there was a reward. If the problem was solvable, the reward would always be behind the black card. If it wasn't, it meant there was no rule that governed which card concealed the reward; the reward

---

*Glass and Singer, cited by Seligman, Martin E. P., *Helplessness: On Depression, Development, and Death.* San Francisco: N.H. Freeman and Co., 1975.
**Hiroto and Seligman, cited by Seligman, Martin E. P., loc. cit.

was distributed arbitrarily. Next the subjects were supposed to turn off an unpleasant noise. Those of the subjects who had previously been given the solvable problems quickly turned off the noise; the others simply put up with it. There is a similar effect when people are rewarded without having done anything to deserve it. It doesn't matter whether a consequence is positive or negative; the important thing is whether one recognizes its connection with one's own behavior. Rewards given randomly without a discernible pattern have an inhibitory effect similar to that of random, uncontrolled punishment.

In the experiment, students who were rewarded arbitrarily behaved less competitively and withdrew from the game earlier. The others competed much more.

Since women are more likely to receive messages of helplessness during childhood, as adults they are more likely to behave in a passive and helpless way. As girls they played games in which it was important to do things together, to establish harmony; the point was to participate in the game, not to win. Being happy about winning wasn't called for. But modesty is the jewel box in which the will to achieve is kept locked up. Even today the questionable virtue of modesty is encouraged. Adina, who is eleven years old, is jubilant because she got an A in her schoolwork. The teacher asks her not to be so exuberant so that the other students won't be disappointed. The boys always go wild when they get good marks, but the teacher has never admonished *them* to be quiet. For girls it is bad to be visibly better than boys. But getting poor grades is also bad. And so Adina is caught in a trap.

Since people tend to generalize from their experiences, that is, to transfer them into other areas of their lives, the experience of being helpless is far-reaching.

Generalizing simplifies life because one doesn't have to figure out how to handle each new situation as it comes along, but rather one can fall back on experience. That is an advantage. But unfortunately, in this way negative processes are also stabilized.

Eventually a single success won't be enough to undo helpless behavior, whereas the repeated experience of lack of control over events will lead to chronic impairment of one's ability to react.*

It was shown experimentally that being unable to control events (learned helplessness) gave rise to the following:**

1. The motivation to act is inhibited.
2. The ability to recognize successes is impaired.
3. There is an increased tendency to react emotionally.

If you compare this with the stereotypes about women, namely that they are submissive, passive, not very ambitious, easily hurt, highly emotional, have little interest in natural science and mathematics, then the correlation is shockingly obvious.

If we assume that helpless behavior can be *unlearned,* we have to ask ourselves how to begin the unlearning process most effectively. The goal is to firmly establish the new experience. You must convince yourself: I can exercise an influence over everything in my life. But since people who have been made helpless are extremely passive, the main hurdle is to get them to start at all. As a first step, they must be made to act, often even forced into action. They have to relearn how to act. Even though, basically, they are convinced that *it is all useless anyway,* they must act against this conviction. There is great danger if they fail, for it would confirm their helplessness. Sad to say, even success is often interpreted negatively.

Luckily, positive experiences are just as resistant to change. A person who believes that her actions can influence the outcome of certain situations will not easily be shaken.

On the other hand, most people have had the experience that although they feel secure in a familiar situation, under different circumstances they can feel quite insecure and helpless.

Usually the expectation alone that an event is beyond one's

---

*Seligman, loc. cit.
**Seligman, loc. cit.

control is enough to cause helplessness. Just as the prediction that an event *is* controllable may be sufficient to motivate a person to react.

Thus students couldn't find the solution to solvable problems after they had first been assigned unsolvable ones by their teacher. But they could do the identical problems without any difficulties for a *different* teacher.*

Similarly, helplessness is more easily transferred from important events to minor ones, rather than the other way around. If, after intensive preparation for a final exam, you've botched it, you tend to expect to fail less important assignments too, whereas doing poorly on a minor test seldom leads to a bad final exam.

Depression as a Reaction to Helplessness

Depression is often a result of not reacting, of inactivity, lack of initiative, inability to act. These are symptoms that also indicate learned helplessness. Frequently depressive people are unable to get anything done; they neglect their appearance; they are apathetic, tired, and indifferent. They prefer being alone, drag themselves around, can't make decisions, feel empty, burned-out, and without any will of their own.

If you look at this negatively, then it paints an exaggerated picture of femininity. One could also call these *traits* exaggerated reticence, passivity, conformity, and insecurity.

Depressive individuals cannot cope with everyday life. On the same level, women are supposed to act charmingly helpless. They are supposed to be dependent and let themselves be cared and provided for by their husbands. They are supposed to feel secure only in the familiar surroundings of their own homes and in *his* presence.

This demand to be feminine initiates the development of learned helplessness and depression.

Depression occurs more often among women than men. It goes along with the symptoms mentioned above and often includes in-

---

*Seligman, loc. cit.

adequate social skills. This is a handicap also described by women who have been out of the workforce for quite a while. Only one or two years after giving up their jobs, women said they could no longer express themselves verbally, they didn't have the nerve to approach people they hadn't met before, and were afraid of social contacts. They just wanted to stay home.

Depressive people think they are less capable than they really are. Even women who are not depressive feel this way about themselves. They believe they are unattractive and stupid. They think they can't do anything on their own; they always expect to fail. Depressive women as well as depressive men account for their successes and failures in similar ways.

People who are not depressive credit their successes to their skills. In contrast, depressive subjects in an experiment were convinced that what they did had as little effect on tasks requiring some skill as on working out unsolvable problems.

The road out of helplessness always leads by way of the experience—pushed or forced on one—that one's own attitude and behavior can have positive consequences.

Everyone is happy when he senses that his behavior has caused something to happen. It starts when a baby feels it is causing the rattle to make a sound. And the signals are set when the baby is allowed to hold its own bottle and learns to satisfy its needs. Parents who make it possible for their children to learn through experience (1) that there is a connection between a certain behavior and its consequence, and (2) that when they do something it will have a certain result, will keep their children from feeling helpless.

If children don't learn to cope with frustration, or if adults smooth out all difficulties for them, helplessness is nurtured. Learned helplessness in children is a serious matter because any motivation to learn and to solve problems independently is nipped in the bud. Girls are especially affected by this, particularly in the mathematical and scientific-technical fields. After a series of failures, most of them give up. This form of resignation to one's fate is quite common among girls. For example, Beth stopped raising her hand in math class. "The teacher," she said, "doesn't think much of girls; anyway, she doesn't call on me." You can only overcome helplessness when you can explain failures and give exact reasons for them.

Do you often have the impression that you blame your failures on personal shortcomings? Then try putting the blame on external circumstances, on someone else, or on the fact that you're having a bad day.

Good girls have learned always to blame themselves. Bad girls blame someone else, the situation, or the weather. I don't want you to be unrealistic in putting the responsibility on others. What matters is that you realize there are other patterns for explaining failures—*and* that tomorrow everything is bound to be different.

People have to learn as early as possible that, through their own behavior, they can cope with anger, monotony, pain, and difficulties. Unfortunately, girls are often *overprotected*. As a result, they have scarcely any opportunities to learn that they can handle difficult situations.

The childhood experience of being able to effectively exercise control is like an immunization against helplessness in adulthood.*

And precisely this experience is withheld from girls.

It's more complicated to acquire such protection in adulthood. First the "illness" has to be cured. It takes a whole series of "immunizing stimulants," that is, experiences that prove: "I can actually overcome difficulties and surmount obstacles." Such "counterexperiences" must be cumulative so that the protection will work for a long time.

Once it's been undermined by helplessness, the will to actively make your own decisions can only be revived slowly.

Adults can get rid of their feeling of helplessness by looking for experiences that will prove to them that they *can* affect circumstances. Perhaps they can remember episodes from the past in

---

*Seligman, loc. cit.

which they implemented change. This requires alterations in our patterns of behavior. You can pick out successes and failures relatively quickly. It is harder to recognize the microstructure of our behavior—the subtleties of gestures, mimicry, and language—and to change it.

Chapter 6

Helpless
Smiles

·

Submissive Body Language

Women use all kinds of body language to say, "I'm small and help-less. I'm no threat to you." They take shorter steps than men; they take up less room; they make themselves "thin."

In more than two thousand photographs taken by one photographer, women hold their arms close to their bodies, carefully placing one foot in front of the other as they walk. On a sandy beach, you can see that a woman's footprints proceed in a nearly straight line. But now look at men's footprints: The left foot and the right foot clearly come down on either side of that line. If you exaggerate the two styles of walking, the advantages and disadvantages are obvious. Women walk with little mincing steps; their balance is precarious and a little wobbly. Men move with broad open strides and sure steps.

The way women sit also shows them trying to make themselves thin. They sit with their arms pressed against their bodies, legs and knees close together, and feet next to each other or pointing inward. Men—with only a few exceptions—almost never assume this posture.

Before puberty there is hardly any difference between the postures of boys and girls. Apparently, as they begin to mature, girls adapt their behavior and body language to the demands of their environment. After a period of rebellion, they become "better behaved," more modest, and more timid, and their body language changes accordingly.

Fashion, too, supports a man in his casual, expansive movements: generously cut jackets and trousers that allow men to nonchalantly place their right leg over their left knee; flat, wide shoes that permit a secure stance and firm step. In contrast, women's shoes are intended to make the foot appear smaller, always at the expense of comfort and sure footing. Women's clothes restrict and confine. That even goes for wide skirts, which, although they permit some freedom of movement, make it difficult to run.

⚠

Ask a woman friend to sit down on a chair facing you. Observe how she sits. Try to figure out what her posture expresses. Note how she places her legs: Do you see the message it sends? Ask your friend how she feels sitting there like that. Next, ask her to sprawl on the chair, or in an easy chair, relaxed, with legs spread apart. Tell her to take up all the available space. Then figure out the message this position sends. Now ask your friend again how she feels. What do you think when you see a woman sitting like this? Now, play this game yourself, and take time to figure out how <u>you</u> feel doing this.

Next, repeat the process with a man:

Ask a male friend to sit down and do the same things. Then ask him to sit like a woman with his eyes slightly downcast. Tell him to exaggerate a little, press his legs close together, at a slant, hold his arms close to his body. How do you like this man now? Go ahead, ask him how he feels.

You can also do experiments in walking—try little mincing steps, one foot in front of the other (to help you exaggerate, think of a model traipsing down the runway in a fashion show); and then try generous, broad-legged steps.

You often hear men making fun of the odd way so many women walk, with their pelvis pushed slightly forward, knees close together, feet and legs splaying out backwards. It really does look quite peculiar. Even when a woman walks, she keeps her legs together. Not only does it look ridiculous, but it hampers her. It's terribly strenuous, she trips more easily, and she can't walk very fast.

Tall women have an additional problem; they not only try to make themselves thin, but also shorter. Wearing low-heeled shoes, they develop various strategies to look like dolls. They push their pelvis to one side, and contort themselves sideways into an S shape, all just so that a man standing next to them won't appear short. They scrunch their shoulders together, lower their heads, and then shyly look up—like turtles.

In a weekend body-language workshop, Charlene told about a fight she had had with her husband. She is taller than he is. Yet standing next to him, she feels short—like a schoolgirl beside her teacher. She is easily intimidated by him because he is loud and aggressive. Whenever they have an argument, she feels helpless. In the workshop, when she acted out her own part with a shorter woman, members of the group were astonished: Charlene, who was at least half a head taller than the other woman, appeared shorter.

Charlene stood with her legs close together, her eyes cast down as though she were ashamed of something, her head bowed and turned sideways. She spoke with a soft, whining voice—but with her head bent down like that, she could scarcely have done otherwise. Her right arm hung diagonally in front of her body, her right hand touching her left thigh. With her left hand she held on to her right elbow, hunching her shoulders forward. One shoulder sloped down a bit; it looked as though her chin and mouth were about to disappear. Her breathing was shallow. By compressing her rib cage, she was choking off the air to her lungs. Charlene felt like a little disobedient dog who isn't sure what's going to happen to it. Next I gave her an opportunity to take on a different role: I asked her to remember a situation in which she had felt sure of herself. She described an argument she once had with a woman colleague. They both wanted to take a computer course, but their boss would allow only one of them to enroll. And he wanted *them* to decide who should go. Charlene was sure that she ought to have the chance. She described how she had discussed the matter with her colleague, her head held high, as though defending her turf. She had vigorously justified her interests and presented her arguments with a steadfast gaze.

While she was telling the story she assumed the position she was describing. She stood up straight, looking directly at the woman participating in the dramatization. She put one hand into her pants pocket and let the other dangle. Still carefully smiling, she seemed considerably more secure. She had straightened her posture, and we could see that she was really tall. Her aim in smiling was completely different now. She was using her smile to calm the woman acting opposite her; she thought if she didn't smile, it would scare her.

The other women in the workshop told Charlene that she not only seemed more self-assured now, but that they believed she would also be able to make an "aggressive" impression in the real world.

That's just what Charlene was afraid of. She didn't want to be seen as ruthless. Her grandmother used to warn her to be more quiet and reticent, that with her loud and direct manner, she'd frighten off other people, and then she shouldn't be surprised if nobody wanted to have anything to do with her. As long as she treated people that way, her grandmother said, she'd never land a husband.

This Is How Women Often Sit:

Legs crossed, close together, at a slant. Add to that a pair of high heels. This is an image most people think of as sexy.

Women usually sit in one corner of a sofa. Men almost always spread out, taking up space. Women seldom encroach on another person's space, in contrast to men who appropriate territory, especially where women make it easy for them. Women don't defend their turf.

Girls, when they have barely outgrown their kiddie shoes, begin to learn cute gestures that diminish and belittle them.

A ten-year-old girl was sprawled comfortably in an armchair. A friend of her father coming into the room set her straight. "Girls don't sit that way," he reproached her, but failed to explain how girls were *supposed* to sit. (He also ignored the mother's wary comment that, after all, the child was wearing pants.) Nevertheless, the girl immediately assumed a position that made her seem smaller, younger, better behaved, and almost shy. She knew what was expected: sit up straight, make yourself thin, keep your legs close together. Both her father and his friend smiled good-naturedly and nodded approval.

Many women know all about these postures—they learned them in dance class if not before. Whether women wear pants or not, they're expected to take up little room. And they comply. When they spread out, they feel vaguely uneasy and strange.

The reason behind these rules is obvious: Just once, in a group discussion, while you're swaying on high heels, your legs close together, your head down and throat throttled, try to get the floor and convince others of your ideas.

Women look especially "cute" when they smile charmingly and incline their heads sideways, like a good little dog. It's a pose that says: "I'm timid; I don't know whether I'm doing everything right."

Tilting the head like that and smiling is something you see almost exclusively in women. It's a sign of meekness. With this pose she is getting ready to graduate from the School for Subservience. With affected gestures she meets the requirement to be lovely, sweet, and affectionate. With a coy gesture she brushes the hair off her forehead; she crosses and uncrosses her legs restlessly, she shyly arranges her skirt, and gently runs her hands over her thighs. She seems to be saying: I'm just a purring kitten; I'll never use my claws.

The Invisible Woman

Many women try to follow these prescriptions to be inconspicuous, unobtrusive, modest, and quiet. It's as though they have put on a magic hat that makes them invisible. They smile and restrain themselves. Instead of contributing their own opinions, they listen patiently to spiels by long-winded talkers without interrupting them.

At one of my seminars where people come to find out whether others see them as they see themselves, there are always several women who seem pale, small, and shy—wallflowers. The others in the class scarcely know how to deal with these women. But often, behind this kind of mask, there's a sharp and observant woman who judges the other participants incisively, without pulling any punches. Of course, she would never say anything until she's asked to speak. Normally she wouldn't even be asked for her opinion. Her posture, the way she looks at you, the clothes she wears, all say: "I'm a nobody. I don't have anything to say. And even if I did, it might be wrong or boring. I don't want to be unfair to anybody; let me be."

Mary Lou was one of these unobtrusive women. She sat leaning forward and hunched over, her back bent, her head pulled in. Her eyes were cast down, and she seemed to be trying not to look anybody in the eye or to be "caught" looking up.

Her clothes spelled modesty—conservative in style, muted colors, with only two "brave" spots of color: some bright trinkets on her shoes and a red-lettered slogan on her T-shirt. Her movements seemed feeble, "anemic," as though she might faint at any moment. This is the impression such women make when you first look at them. But once they start to speak and when they sense that their audience is pleasantly surprised, they get going.

They become cheerful, often even sarcastic, and you get an inkling of what they're really made of: They have bite and power and the ability to form opinions. Unfortunately, they are so afraid of this side of their personalities that after their outburst, they just want to sink into the ground. They're afraid of being rejected and criticized if they express their opinions. And sad to say, they do encounter such rebuffs. Their external appearance just doesn't jibe with their incisive statements. You simply don't expect them to be so sharp. Also, it has something to do with the suddenness and often unsuitable gruffness of their outbursts. For when someone who has been calm and silent for a long time suddenly steps out of the shadows, she may easily overreact. And that is sure to meet with a quick response. The target of her outburst, of course, is shocked and defends himself. So her "boldness" is nipped in the bud before it has a chance to unfold.

Here's Looking at You, Kid

Expressing more than a thousand words, the eyes of many women convey their willingness to be submissive. Their looks reflect a shy, timid inner life. Because they're afraid they might scare off other people or hurt their feelings by staring at them, women carefully glance to the side or downward in embarrassment. They don't want you to feel they are staring at you, because that would stir up animosity. Everyone knows how uncomfortable it is to be stared at continuously; it makes you feel insecure, embarrassed, even anxious. And who doesn't know the little game wherein two people stare at each other, and the one who doesn't blink is the winner.

Being stared at is unpleasant, and you try to escape from it. In an experiment, drivers waiting for a traffic light to change drove off more quickly if someone was staring at them. You even hear children defend themselves: "Don't look at me like that," or "Why are you staring at me like that?" The one who is staring wants something, and the person being stared at has the gut feeling "Nothing good will come of this!"

Staring is a threatening gesture. Cats do it; if you get the chance, watch how they snarl while staring fixedly into each other's eyes. People also feel threatened by stares. The one who's weaker slinks away; the powerful one stays. Take Ingrid Bergman in *Casablanca*. She looks up at Humphrey Bogart with a shy glance; she can only look into his eyes modestly, through a film of tears. At least in the animal world, this has the effect of reducing direct physical violence. A male gorilla would kill a female who stared at him too long.

Women are often stared at. Sometimes in admiration, often in a deprecatory way, but usually lecherously. Justifiably, they feel threatened and uncomfortable. Whether they turn away in embarrassment or smile, they consistently signal submission rather than readiness to fight. They are surprised that their shy smiles don't soothe or distract anybody. They feel threatened, but don't dare chase away the potential "attacker" with a withering look or a sharp remark. The person who can stare or return a stare is powerful. The submissive one looks away, hoping in this way to avoid an aggressive or coercive act.

Perhaps the starer only wants to make contact and to signal: "I'm interested in you; I like you." It's hard to differentiate between these two possibilities; looks are seldom clear and unambiguous. They can only be interpreted in connection with other body signals, with verbal language, and in the context of a particular situation. Presumably women who dare to look at a man "too long" are encouraging him; they are inviting him to speak to them.

Women are considered beautiful if they have big, wide-open eyes. It makes them look surprised and harmless. During adolescence girls practice this Bambi look. They gaze at the world with big eyes and slightly opened mouths, not realizing that not only do they look harmless, but also stupid. You can't stare someone down or drive him off with that doe-eyed look; it just doesn't work. During this same period boys practice how to look people "coolly" in the eye. Being cool means to hide your feelings, to control yourself, and not display any weak spots. A cool guy doesn't lose his composure, doesn't get hysterical, and holds the reins of power casually in his hand. Men are cool, and cool little boys are going to have the right to exercise male power someday.

Girls show their feelings and so they're "not cool." No poker faces for them; anyone can see how they feel. As one young woman said about herself: "I have an honest face. It gives me away; I can't bluff." She thinks these qualities are desirable virtues, but also a handicap. She suspects that people don't take her seriously, and that, she thinks, is a personal flaw.

Bosses, on the other hand, are cool. Only those who have power decide when to tell, show, or reveal something and to whom. It's easy to make unimportant, dependent people who wear their hearts on their sleeves feel insecure. They answer promptly every time they're asked a question, and they smile.

Tell Me if I'm Doing It Right

Studies show that a woman will look at another person more often and longer than a man will. But she watches without staring. She turns her eyes away as soon as she senses that the other person is getting uncomfortable or that he, in turn, is now looking into *her* eyes. This may be because women take their cues from the other person and adjust their behavior in accordance with his anticipated reactions. They look at other people in order to "read" their expectations early on, if possible before they are even expressed.

Since a woman today is often still materially and/or emotionally dependent on a man, it is important for her security and well-being to rapidly recognize what is expected of her. A woman first looks for clues as to how she should behave. Then by making brief eye contact she checks to see whether what she did was all right.

Trying to make eye contact can certainly be a sign of submissiveness. For instance, a weaker woman wants to keep an eye on a stronger man to check on his mood so that she can intervene in time to placate him or flee, to adapt or to simply look for his approval.

How often have you looked at someone to find out whether she or he approves or disapproves of your actions? Looking at someone says, "I'm listening to you. What you say is important to me." Looking at a person is sending him an effective sign that you are paying attention and are interested in him and what he is saying. But it turns into a handicap when it is one-sided. Women are the listening gender, and good women are always ready to lend an ear. They are sympathetic and show their willingness with understanding glances.

Men have a hungry look. It signals that they will take what they want. Men ogle women brazenly, and women furtively avert their eyes. But as soon as a woman looks at a man that way, she is accused of a sexual "come-on" or aggressiveness.

Try this:
   Take a walk through town and look passersby directly in the eye. Don't smile; just look at them. Gauge your feelings. What sensations do you have?

Go to a bar with a girlfriend and take a good look at the men who are there. Look them up and down. Be aware of your feelings while you're doing this, *and* observe the reactions of the men.

Dressing to Express Submissiveness

What you wear indicates your attitude and social status. Don't you judge other people as well-off or poor on the basis of their clothes? How a person is dressed invites us to judge his character, his abilities, and his intelligence. You can use this to effect by dressing up or down. "Clothes make the man" is a cliché that is applicable today more than ever. When women first tried to get higher-level managerial jobs, they often did so in suits that strongly resembled masculine styles.

As I've said before: Women's clothes, even today, are often uncomfortably tight and restrict mobility. Even wide clothes are cut so that women can get entangled in them.

Little girls, too, are dressed so they can't move around freely. Patent leather shoes are still "in" today. The soles are smooth, and running in these shoes often ends in falls. Little girls are spiffed up in spic-and-span skirts and pants, and not allowed to get them dirty. They're admonished, "Careful, watch what you're doing." Girls are supposed to be careful and reticent in all areas of life. Clothes "make it easier" for little ladies to toe that line. By the time they grow up, they hardly notice the shackles anymore.

At this point I want to touch on the subject of power again, the ability to make decisions and to act. I mean power as a personality trait, an inner strength that, depending on the individual, comes across in different ways. Only if you are brave enough to strengthen your own personality can you have the power to influence other people positively and convincingly. But you can only develop your personality in this way if you concentrate on your own desires and needs. Women who are constantly worrying about what others think of them, what the neighbors are saying, and whether people like them or not cannot develop a strong, confident personality. And that also goes for those women who are always trying to follow the rules and who adapt to particular situations, in dress and behavior.

Brenda and her husband had lived abroad for many years. She had worked as an executive secretary there, and now that they were back home, she started looking for a job. When she went for an interview, she felt that, in addition to her business expertise, she could also sell her personality. She wore her most expensive suit and jewelry.

Brenda was certain she would get the job thanks to her knowledge of foreign languages, her professional competence, and, not least, her elegant getup.

A week later, when she received a polite rejection letter, she was taken aback.

We discussed the situation, and it soon turned out that the man who would have been her boss couldn't have held a candle to her. She said that as soon as she entered his office she saw that he certainly couldn't give his wife the luxuries her own husband afforded her. The office was solidly and expensively furnished; he was suitably dressed; but it was all far below the level she was accustomed to. Brenda didn't realize that she was describing exactly what had gone wrong in the interview. She thought he should have been glad to get her as an employee. Obviously she had sent him the unspoken message "I'm up here, you're down there."

Brenda had to get it through her head that whoever her future boss is, he'll have more power than she. And she has to show him that she will accept his authority. During the interview she had let it be known, although not in so many words, that the job did not correspond to her standards. So of course, she didn't get it. She was indignant when I advised her to dress more modestly for future job interviews: "Women aren't supposed to make themselves small and give up their demands," she objected. "After all, that's what *you're* always preaching, and now I'm supposed to do just the opposite?" She was clearly annoyed. Of course, Brenda isn't supposed to renounce having power and influence, but she has to recognize how far she can go in her job. She must be confident enough to accept the existing power structure at her workplace. She can try for a higher position once she's demonstrated her expertise. But if she overdoes it at the outset by wearing the wrong clothes, she won't get the chance.

The Language of Submission

There are lots of words "decent girls don't use." This is where verbal submission begins, if not earlier.

Women demonstrate the subtlest kind of submissiveness in the language they use. It's difficult to put your finger on it and categorize it precisely, and yet it is extremely effective. Recently Deborah Tannen made many readers aware of how distinctly different female and male language are.* Although this may not be proof of the submissiveness of female language, still Tannen's research contains hints pointing in that direction. I would like to differentiate among four clearly defined patterns of verbal submission.

Omissions
Insufficient Insistence

---

*Tannen, Deborah, *You Just Don't Understand: Women and Men in Conversation*. New York: Ballantine Books, 1990.

Retraction
Guessing Games

As for *omissions,* there are many things women don't say, or they don't say them the way they mean them.

Insufficient insistence deals with the female pattern of making assertions sound more like irrelevancies or questions.

Retraction or taking things back is a technique that supplements lack of insistence. Women tag on seemingly innocent phrases to many of their requests or statements—their main message being "Probably someone else is right."

Verbal self-abnegation in the form of a *guessing game* is especially difficult to recognize in female language patterns: "Please read between the lines and guess what I really want." Women hide or disguise their wishes, expectations, demands, and criticism—to the point that they become unrecognizable.

Omissions

To a large extent people consider swearing, strong language, and sexual suggestiveness off limits for good girls. This kind of language is *still* largely the province of men. It's considered unfeminine to use aggressive or smutty terms. Scarcely a head turns when a man says, "Oh, shit!" But everybody looks up when a woman says it. Yet women hardly notice that they avoid using strong, vulgar language; they rarely let off steam in this fashion. Sometimes you just feel like cursing; and like everyone else, women also feel relieved after they've done it. Often women clam up because they want to avoid conflicts; they'd rather not say anything than say something offensive.

Instead of contradicting men in an argument, a woman sulks and withdraws. At best she'll tell a friend—another woman—what she really thinks. When she's reached an incipient stage of rebellion, she may joke about these men. But unfortunately, jokes are the only weapons the weak have against the powerful. For the time being, peace is maintained, and concealed aggressions are discharged without having done any damage.

Insufficient Insistence

But even when a woman does speak up, she seldom takes a clear position; she would rather leave several possibilities open.

She's afraid to commit herself because she thinks she will have to stick to what she says. To explain his inconsistency and wavering, a man will say, "What do I care about the stupid things I said yesterday?" But that doesn't work for a woman. When she changes her mind, she's called moody. And so a woman tends to tone down her choice of words and her intonation when she speaks. Her statements end with little questions, even when she is sure of herself and what she's talking about: "Don't you agree?"—"Am I right?"

In this fashion, women try to stabilize their relationships. The primary principle is "Don't step on anybody's toes." This is more important to a woman than to insist on her own ideas. Women create an image of themselves that fits the ideas their partners, friends, parents, and/or children have of them. They don't use a personal language, a way of expressing themselves that fits them individually. The course for their submissive language is set early on. Girls don't acquire the same language patterns as boys. Girls ask or suggest whereas boys are more bossy. Typically girls might say, "Should we do this or that?" Boys will often say, "I want to do this." You hear adult women using careful phrasing like "What would you think if . . ." or when there's a lot of submissiveness involved, "If no one objects, perhaps we could . . ." or "If no one has any other suggestions, then . . ." No wonder there is so much holding back. At most a boy gets a chiding smile for saying, "But I want . . ." However, a girl, trained to speak in a submissive manner, is corrected, "You should say, 'I would like' or 'May I.' "

A teacher once described his problem female students for me. Criticizing one girl because she was self-centered, he said she was pushy in class and always wanted to be called on. That seemed to him not right—for a girl. He described another girl as being enamored with herself. (This seemed bad to him!) The teacher considered this young girl's healthy self-confidence inappropriate. She held her head up and looked him in the eye when he criticized or corrected her, and she asked him to explain his evaluations or demands. He thought that girls should be quiet and reticent. Inappropriate behavior by the boys was more or less condoned, but the girls were penalized.

Moreover, girls—even before puberty—are seen as the weaker gender even though in fifth and sixth grade they are usually taller and stronger than the boys. In gym class the "strong boys" were supposed to set up and take down the equipment. The girls felt this was discrimination. One day the girls rebelled and proved that they were stronger than the boys. Despite that, in the next gym class they were back to the same old routine. Even though the girls had shown they were stronger, the boys wanted to prove their "male" superiority by setting up the equipment. They fought against letting the girls do it.

Subordination through language is, of course, much more complex than my outline suggests. Between *insufficient insistence* and *retraction* we find the frequently used female ploy of refusing to exert any influence, that is, asking rather than urging. "What shall we do?"—"Where are we going this evening?"—"Which movie or television program are you interested in?"—"What would you like me to cook?" This renunciation is so universal that I haven't yet found a woman who has completely abandoned this language pattern.

Retraction

Many women speak tentatively. Every statement may be followed by a quick retraction if somebody doesn't want to go along with what they said. Two favorite words with these women are *maybe* and *perhaps:* Would you *perhaps* bring me the files? *Maybe* we could go to the swimming pool? Do you *perhaps* have time today? The words *perhaps* and *maybe* could easily be left out without changing the meaning of these sentences. They only serve to weaken a question so that it won't sound like a demand.

The words *actually* and *really* have a similar effect. *Actually* I don't feel like it. I *really* want to go home now. *Actually* I already have a date. The way they are used here, *actually* and *really* are words of reversal because, to be precise, a sentence with *actually* or *really* is turned into its opposite: I *really* don't feel like it—but I'll do it anyway. *Actually* I already have a date—but you can try to persuade me. I *actually* wanted to go home now—but I'll stay. In the end, each sentence says: "I am prepared to subordinate myself." Yet hardly anyone is aware of the reversal.

I play a useful game in therapy sessions: Whenever someone says "actually," I ask, "Don't you mean, *not* actually?" If you play this little game with yourself, it might lead you to make a change.

These reversal words are also used by women in public discussions. For example, say a woman wants to put an idea up for discussion. She makes the proposal in all seriousness, and would be hurt if it were simply dismissed. But her own excessive caution in expressing herself and her self-retraction scarcely bother her; in fact, she is hardly aware of them. The dual message, "I would like to, but I am quite ready to come down a peg or two!" is interpreted by her opponent to his own advantage, and rightly so. We'd all go crazy if each time we had to ask, "Exactly how did you mean that sentence? Did you want to or didn't you?" or even worse, if we expected the other person to see through the speaker's fuzzy imprecision and ambiguity.

Who Talks More, Women or Men?

Women also restrain themselves in connection with how long they speak. They imply, "I don't need much time to say this, I am not important, I don't have anything important to say." Everybody says women talk a lot; talking is their favorite pastime. Yet if you observe women at meetings, you'll see that they talk a lot less than the men and they require less time to say what they have to say.

Deborah Tannen describes research into the speaking patterns of men and women in mixed groups (at university faculty meetings).* The results showed that women spoke from three to ten sec-

---

*Tannen, Deborah, op. cit., p. 75.

onds; the men, from eleven to seventeen seconds. The longest contributions by women were still shorter than the shortest by men. Women ought to relish the results of this research in light of the stereotype about female talkativeness. But the fact that women talk more and longer as soon as no men are present in a group casts a long shadow over the female desire for emancipation. In my seminars, too, it is usually the men who make long speeches, who digress, and whom I have to interrupt in order to get them back to the seminar subject. In my public speaking seminars I assign participants to write a speech in which they praise themselves. Men find this much easier to do than women. Men enjoy this assignment and go all out bragging about themselves. Women tend to find the assignment embarrassing. Given a choice, they'd rather pick another subject. Is praising yourself really so bad? Evidently women seem to think so.

At an assessment center session where job candidates were being tested for managerial potential a man took over the leadership of a leaderless group discussion. He was not challenged. (The session—four women, two men—dealt with personnel selection. Participants had to prove, among other things, that they were capable of leadership, good at convincing others, cooperative, etc.) He did this even though nobody approved of him as discussion leader and two of the women were clearly more competent and showed better team spirit.

At the conclusion of the discussion, all the participants agreed that one of the women would have been selected had the group voted on who should be the leader. One woman was sure that "if this man hadn't been there, I would have taken over the leadership. I just didn't want to show him up; that's why I held back." Well, it probably wasn't all that noble. This woman was surely also afraid to deal with conflict publicly, afraid of confrontation, and, not least, afraid of possible defeat. Fear presumably protects you from making a fool of yourself. A person who gives in to fear is passive and therefore cannot make any mistakes. A woman's decision to back down is not always determined by her desire for conciliation and harmony; the risk of an open confrontation plays just as important a role.

Guessing Games

Erica wants to go to the movies, but what she asks her boyfriend is "Would you like to go to a bar, or would you rather go to see a movie?" Her friend is supposed to guess what she wants. She doesn't really want to hide her preference, but uses an abbreviated version of "I would like to go to the movies, but if you'd rather go to a bar, I'd be willing to go along. Of course, I'd like it if you'd go to the movies with me, but I won't be mad at you if you'd rather do something else." Her message is "I will go along with your wishes, but I'll be disappointed."

When women express themselves, they often do so in imprecise, ambiguous language that always leaves them a way out or makes an about-face possible. They challenge others to guess what *they* really mean or want to say.

Not coming out and saying what you really mean—expecting the other person to "read between the lines" of what you say—reveals your uncertainty and makes it much easier for the other person to assert his own opinion. Sometimes he doesn't even realize what you wanted since it was never clearly stated.

Pretending to Be Dumb

Women pretend they are dumb. They let people help them with things, making a big fuss in situations wherein they could easily, with a little effort, help themselves. In this way they enhance the status of the helper and at the same time they subordinate themselves to his intelligence. This also applies to asking for a hand with odd jobs for which presumably male strength is required. Men often take on the role of teachers. They will explain technical, political, economic matters, even if the woman knows as much about the subject or could get the information herself. They demonstrate how things work. They attempt to repair washing machines, even though they don't have the foggiest idea how to service them.

A woman hides her knowledge in the deceptive hope that it will make men like her. She subordinates herself to men by pretending to be stupid. A woman will give men the chance to show off and receive her gratitude in exchange for help that she didn't really need or that was ineffectual anyway.

This form of subordination through feigned ignorance and incompetence is bad enough in everyday life, but at work it becomes a dangerous stumbling block for a woman.

Attempting to obtain the affection of others by pretending to be dumb, and hoping for recognition and success by acting ignorant, are bound to end in failure. What boss would promote a woman who pretends to be stupid? The women who are successful are the ones who take things into their own hands, who work out problems on their own, and who see difficulties as a challenge to show their own mettle and to prove themselves, instead of opening opportunities for others to show off.

But even women who can already do all this unconsciously trip themselves up by smiling modestly and reticently even while they are doing or saying important things.

Chapter 7

Just Keep
Smiling

•

Do We Betray Ourselves with Our Smiles?

Rhoda, thirty-four, is furious. "I'm sick and tired of this damned smile!" she yells at the television monitor. She is participating in a seminar about body language for women. Angrily she studies her own smiling face on the screen.

"This stupid grin. I've been grinning pleasantly at everybody for the last thirty years, even if they've put one over on me or behaved like a cad." Rhoda wants to change, to get out of this mold. "There's something sick about being friendly and keeping my cool even when I'm treated badly," she says. Up to now she's considered it a sign of weakness to let on that someone has hurt or annoyed her. She'd grit her teeth and smile. "I could never quite understand why my stomach rebelled in situations like that. And why I'd be lying in bed at night, crying and not knowing just what it was that got me down." Now she knows. "It's this damned smiling, this face that tells everybody, 'I'm not mad at you; please don't turn away from me.' I should have cursed, screamed, gone on a rampage and smashed dishes, or just turned on my heels and disappeared for good."

Many women feel this way. They realize they are betraying themselves with their friendly smiles and are sacrificing themselves. Yet they think it's the only way to achieve their goals, or the only way not to lose face in a delicate situation. They don't really defend themselves, not even when they're being treated badly. And more often than most of them would like to admit, it's the secret worry that they'll be rejected that forces a smile to their lips. This smile isn't an expression of joy; rather it reflects their concern about being able to retain the affection of the people around them. "Please like me, don't hurt me, don't leave me" is the message these smiles send.

If you can, imagine yourself saying, "Go ahead, give me a dirty look. It doesn't bother me if somebody gets angry with me sometimes."

Even if you don't <u>say</u> it, try to <u>think</u> it.

Why Is It Women Who Fall into This Trap?

It isn't easy to explain what causes many women to smile even when they have quite different feelings inside. But before I go into the reasons behind the submissive female smile, I want to clarify my attitude toward smiling in general. Some of you may suspect that I am a pessimistic misanthrope who classifies smiling as sick or always out of place. Quite the contrary. I think smiling is valuable if it reflects inner strength, if it conveys a feeling of power and indicates unequivocally, "I'm listening and I like you." Then a smile is the sign of a free and conscious decision; it is something important and beautiful. Unfortunately, we often *don't* smile with that in mind, but fall into the Mona Lisa trap. Whenever women smile even though they are not in a happy mood, they're walking smack into this trap. (More about that later.)

Why Do Women Often Smile So Submissively?

Women may have equal rights, but they are not yet independent in the true sense of the word. They have only formally liberated themselves from the oppressed gender role they have played for thousands of years. In their minds the oppression continues. They cling to the obsequious tactics oppressed people have always used to pursue their goals. It makes sense to use a strategy of seeming submissive in a rigidly hierarchical society. You simply grin and bear it and follow an indirect path toward your goals. Certainly flattery, manipulation, humility, or self-sacrifice have always been ways to get the recognition and esteem of a ruler. Luckily today's social structures are more open. Modern constitutional provisions have for quite some time postulated gender equality. But women often act as though these regulations do not apply to them, as though it were always necessary to make deals with those in power in order to be entitled to protection.

Today men and women may be competitors, but they are not necessarily enemies. For the time being, men may be a step ahead. As in every game, courage, initiative, and persistence will get results. Or do you expect others to clear the playing field for you? Stop complaining about the rottenness of the world. That won't get you anywhere. What will get you ahead is making a clear-cut decision to do something about your own submissive mind-set, because this unfortunately still governs the behavior of many women, even today. Sometimes it may be subliminal, but in any case it works against your development and growth. It keeps a woman from achieving a healthy feeling of self-worth. I call this self-limiting and self-denying mentality the *Mona Lisa syndrome,* because for me her inscrutable smile is a powerful symbol of female submissiveness.

If you've ever seen the *Mona Lisa,* you probably sensed the melancholy sadness of her smile. It surely is one of the reasons the portrait is so famous. But when I look at that picture I have a sense of unease rather than of admiration. For a long time I didn't know why—until I recognized in that smile something I had often seen in my therapy sessions: the unmistakable sign of female surrender. There is another artistic treatment of this condition that moved me even more deeply. Perhaps you remember the film *The Lacemaker,* which tells of a sensitive girl's consuming love for a man who, after a long, tender, and passionate love affair, turns away and leaves her. Her heart is broken, and in her derangement she also smiles this transfigured, melancholy smile.

In seminars and conferences I have seen women whose smiles had a similar quality. Even after they were humiliated, hurt, or treated badly, a desperate smile was pasted on their faces. It lingered when they spoke of their hopes or of a few beautiful moments in their lives or the happy time at the beginning of their relationship. Their smiles were also desperate because many of these women were sure they would go back to the same partner if he would only reach out to them. Women have to get through some difficult stages of personal growth before they can confidently face their old partner or a new one. It often takes months in therapy until the stored-up hate, almost always hidden behind this patient suffering, works its way up to the surface. Here are a few examples of the underlying reasons for smiling self-submission.

You already know Rhoda, a petite woman whose story is typical of women with the Mona Lisa smile. When she was nineteen years old she met Peter, a twenty-six-year-old engineer, whom she liked right off the bat because he seemed modest and polite. She was relieved that he did not make sexual advances, as other men had done. Rhoda and Peter were engaged for three years, until Peter reached the point professionally when he felt they were "ready to get married." Rhoda had long ago stopped thinking about what she wanted to do or what she felt was right. Peter was somewhat opinionated, but that rarely bothered Rhoda, who thought she suited him just fine. She was always ready to adopt his opinions, especially when he indicated with a rather arrogant, condescending look that the problem could only be solved with logic. Or when something had to do with *superior logic,* and only *he* was in a position to decide what was right or wrong. For Rhoda, *superior logic* became a synonym for her inability to follow his train of thought. She was grateful for having landed a husband with a superior education and tried to remember some of his arguments.

But with time she found that he was very capricious about how he used these arguments. And more and more frequently she realized that what he presented as correct and logical was always the opposite of what she thought. Rhoda concluded she was the one who *in principle* was always wrong. They had two children, although she would have preferred only one. They moved to the suburbs, even though she really wanted to stay in town. Rhoda was shy, and when they moved it was hard for her to lose the only two girlfriends she had. After the move, she rarely got together with her friends because her husband thought she didn't need to have a car of her own in the suburbs. She would have liked to go back to work, but Peter decided that it would be better for the children to have their mother at home. Rhoda kept smiling, but not with her eyes; her eyes were sad.

She was no coward. There were violent rows, often about the children. She would fight passionately for them against her conservative husband. But most of the time he got his way.

She uncomplainingly took care of the household and accepted most of her husband's decisions with little back talk. *After all, he was the one who earned the money.* And even though she was sick and tired of it, she put up with vacationing year after year in the same mountain resort town.

At a certain point, after so much patient endurance, the body just rebels. Rhoda often had stomach cramps, and because she never complained to her doctor, an ulcer developed for which she had to have surgery. She picked the vacation period to go to the hospital because this way her absence would have the least impact on her family. During that vacation Peter met another woman, no younger than Rhoda but more independent and with her own money and interests. Not long after that, he walked out on the family.

As he explained to Rhoda later, he had long ago gotten bored with her, her narrow-mindedness, and her constant smile.

Rhoda is representative of a common female custom of making oneself small and unassuming; her story clearly proves the futility of adapting to her husband's demands to the point that she lost her identity. She wasn't happy, nor did her submissiveness lend her marriage permanence. On the contrary, if you believe her husband, her patience bored him. Be that as it may, smiling subservience brought her nothing. The anger she feels toward herself, which I described at the beginning of this section, is understandable. She is right in thinking that her patience and her good-natured self-sacrifice contributed a lot to her misery. The placid smile she sees on the screen symbolizes her renunciation of power.

Rhoda had sacrificed herself, but that isn't the only common behavior I found among these sadly smiling women. The next chapter presents an outline that can be used to classify and more easily identify their different behaviors.

Does this pussyfooting renunciation seem familiar to you?

Examine your own behavior to see whether you also tend to stay in the background for seemingly rational reasons or out of mistaken consideration for others.

Chapter 8

The
Mona Lisa
Mentality

.

Relationship traps, described later in this chapter, are *relationship structures* that women put up with or set up. However, before a woman can fall into these relationship traps, quite a few things will have gone wrong. Seemingly harmless little mechanisms pave the way to the big traps. That is why Mona Lisa traps can only be completely understood after the basic patterns common to all traps are explained. I call them the Mona Lisa mentality.

There is still another reason to examine these forerunners to the Mona Lisa trap. The more closely I looked at the problem, the more apparent it became that almost every woman has a certain measure of the Mona Lisa mentality within her.

By now you probably know there are degrees of severity here. The Mona Lisa *mentality* is the weakest form of self-abnegation. In the Mona Lisa *traps* there is already a substantial degree of self-surrender at play. But in the Mona Lisa *syndrome* there is probably a real mental problem or illness present. First let me list the typical symptoms of the Mona Lisa mentality:

- Goals are approached circuitously **(fear of conflict).**
- What one's husband or partner or other people think, wish,

or expect is usually considered more important than one's own wishes and goals **(heteronomy).**

- The highest goal is to accommodate everybody else's wishes **(desire for harmony).**
- Frequently other people's interests are tended to before they have even asked for something **(obedience in anticipation).**

A woman who finds herself frequently in *one* of these categories is in danger of heading from the Mona Lisa mentality into the Mona Lisa trap. She is probably acting against her own wishes and goals more often than she would like to or is aware of.

Why do so many women take refuge in these patterns?

Their upbringing teaches them to get results with *feminine tactics* that use feminine gestures and behavior such as: raising their eyes and blinking innocently, acting coy, being motherly and warm. In our society women are traditionally not encouraged to fight or get into serious debates. They grow up with the understanding that in the role of "WOMAN" they will be guaranteed protection from life's challenges as long as they behave according to the role model.

But this expectation can be extremely misleading, for times have changed and many women today have to face the challenges of everyday life alone. In spite of that, many would rather invest their time in choosing what clothes to wear than in taking a course in assertiveness training, learning how to fight, or furthering their education. They hope that beauty and gentleness will open the way to some man's heart and thus a comfortable life. But this hope is bound to lead to disappointment. Men (certainly the New Man) increasingly are looking for equal partners with whom they can argue, and to whom they can hand over responsibility and a share in providing for their joint livelihood. It's gradually dawning on men that having a strong woman as a wife or partner is an advantage in the long run, even though some of the confrontations with her will clearly become more difficult.

Anyone toying with the idea of changing her strategy now and resolving from this moment on to appear strong in order to catch herself a man is still caught in the adaptation trap. The solution isn't getting your man and being loved by hook or by crook; it is to grow into a self-sufficient, self-confident person.

Am I Already Caught in the Trap?

Women caught in the Mona Lisa trap are those who constantly ask, "What would YOU like?" They're continually looking for reassurance for *their* decisions, even when they know precisely what they want and nobody has any serious objections. They ask others to decide for them even when they're the only ones who can make the decision. In seeking help, they're on the lookout for someone who will take their last chance for self-determination out of their hands. Then, at the bitter end, they thank him with a smile for his friendly help and scarcely realize that it was, after all, help to their own self-mutilation.

They adhere to the unspoken precept that any decision made without your partner's approval is a bad decision.

"What would **YOU** like?" becomes synonymous with self-denial, retreat, and lack of self-assertion. Anyone who asks this question frequently is renouncing her independence. She thinks that negotiating or wrangling about something with her argumentative partner is self-centered.

A woman who, despite her fits of hysteria, often doesn't get what she wants is also living a Mona Lisa life.

Naturally there are many women who aren't that deeply mired in the Mona Lisa trap; they defend their opinions and demand that others pay attention to them or do some of the work. But unfortunately, few of them do this without feeling guilty. Almost all the women I talked to said that whenever they made any clear demands, insisted on their own ideas, claimed their rights, or showed aggressive feelings, they always did so with a bad conscience, guilt feelings, or tension.

Women who want to shed their submissive behavior are going to be haunted for a long time by words echoing from their childhood: You mustn't do that; that's not nice; it's not good for you; if everybody were to do that . . .; you'll never reach your goal by making demands; you'll be a laughingstock; you're too bossy; if you're not friendly, nobody will like you.

Women rarely are aware of what they're doing to themselves by behaving as they do. Unintentionally they create a degrading self-image of servitude. A woman who rarely says straight out what she wants, who always looks first to see what other people want or might want, will turn into a servile hypocrite. Smiling won't help.

First, ask yourself, "What do *I* want?"
Put YOUR goals first!
What is it that's different for men?

One might argue, not much; aren't they also oppressed? What is it then that's so special about the smiling oppressed woman?

Of course, men voluntarily or involuntarily submit too, but they rarely smile while they do; more likely they choke back their anger and look grave, dejected, angry, or arrogant.

In principle men can also fall into the Mona Lisa trap. However, it is primarily women who suffer under the patriarchal power structure.

Women who smilingly refuse to express straightforward opinions, who make loud and clear demands, or who hope to achieve with wile what they don't dare to strive for directly are destroying their self-respect. They undermine their social status and delay the day of true equality. It's futile to have a piece of paper granting you a right if you then don't make use of it.

At first glance this may seem like an exaggeration. How is the self-denial of women supposed to have an impact on equal rights?

Unfortunately, however, the attainment of equal rights is being hampered from two directions. On the one side, by men who don't want to share some of their power, and on the other by women who are not demanding any power.

Legislating women's rights achieves little by itself. Equal rights will be a hollow phrase so long as women complain that no one has come along to give them these rights *voluntarily*. Rights have meaning only when they are firmly rooted in the mind **and** when they are demanded. It's hard to believe, but women won't take what they are entitled to.

The following story is true, no matter how improbable it may sound.

The woman co-owner of a medium-sized business wanted to give her employees equal pay for equal work. Even though her company was justly considered women-friendly, she was in a difficult position. The firm's profits were simply not sufficient to bring the women's wages up to the level of the men's; so equalization of pay was to be achieved through restructuring at no additional cost. But the women employees rejected that solution. The men, they said, would rebel if they were going to be paid less. And for that reason the women waived pay equalization. They didn't insist on their rights, preferring to accept it as a given that they would earn less: "It's always been that way," they said. True, a few grumbled that it was a disgrace, but most of the women didn't want any trouble with their male colleagues. So in the end, the owner received no support from her employees on the equal-pay issue.

Unions cannot wring higher wages from employers without making demands or being ready for confrontations. Nor can women expect genuine social power if they don't make clear and—from the male viewpoint—tough demands.

Women have a weak lobby; nobody champions their rights in earnest, not even they themselves. I think that in this context (and not only in this context), women—collectively—are suffering from the Mona Lisa syndrome.

⚠

Imagine that you can achieve your goal by being straightforward rather than with indirect tactics or wiles. Take it as your right to hone in on your own goals and wishes DIRECTLY!

The Wrong Way to Escape the Mona Lisa Trap

This book exists to tackle traditional concepts of femininity. I want to free women from the negative aspects of the cliché because this image has a lot to do with the Mona Lisa trap. The traditional cliché of *femininity* almost obligates a woman to be either patient and yielding or complaining, weeping, and hysterically helpless. Yet in both cases the interests of women are treated as if they were of secondary importance and their opinions are ignored. Women who assume these roles should not be surprised when their ideas are dismissed as childish. Without putting up any great opposition, such women even allow their sexuality to be shoved into one of two categories—"passive-shy" or "man-eating-greedy."

Neither role works. If the following two stories remind you of your own failures, then perhaps you can now understand how the Mona Lisa legacy was (or is) at play in your case too.

The first is an example of an *unsuccessful* attempt.

Ruth and Ted have been married for ten years. One of the things they frequently argue about is that Ruth would like her husband to pick up their daughter Julia at her girlfriend's house. While he's gone, Ruth wants to catch up on some of the housework. Therefore she asks him (somewhat too sweetly):

"Did you have a rough day at work?"

"No!"

"I'm going to do some ironing. Do you feel like picking up Julia?"

"No. *You* do it. I'm hungry and I want a drink. The news is going to be on soon. Anyway, Julia can take the bus home. You're spoiling her."

By now Ruth is seething, but she controls herself and answers, "I think it isn't fair for you to just sit there while I'm stuck with all the work."

Ted stays cool. "No matter what, I won't pick her up. Let her find a way to get home!"

Ruth doesn't calm down until she's sitting in the car on the way to pick up her daughter. For the nth time she's lost one of these arguments. She is furious with herself and her husband. She thinks about getting a divorce. All her self-control and the many desperate attempts to stay calm have been for nothing.

A lot of women are familiar with scenes like this in which they helplessly or sometimes furiously have to back down.

⚠

Can you imagine yourself being furious and indignant about something? How often do <u>you</u> allow yourself to react angrily, vehemently?

Of course, quite a few women have found out that smiles and self-control don't get them anywhere. But all the same, they have had only modest success in winning arguments.

Now, here is an example of a hysterical approach—an aggressive attempt to get one's way—that is just as fruitless:

All the quarrels between Edith and Bruce, who have been married for four years, end the same way: Edith sitting at the kitchen table, crying; Bruce escaping to the corner bar. As usual, Edith had lost the weekly fight over who would clean the bathroom. The arguments always start pretty much the same way. But this time Edith had firmly resolved to get her husband to do some of the work. She had prepared some sound reasons why he should help, even rehearsing what she would say to him. She was quite confident that this time it would work. Then she sat down across from him at the kitchen table. He looked tired, but he realized immediately that the weekly cleaning row was about to begin.

She came to the point right away. "We have to have a talk about cleaning the bathroom."

"Not again!"

"As usual, you're trying to get out of doing your share of the work."

He didn't even think he had to answer her. Fetching a beer out of the fridge, he gave her a challenging look and she lost all her nerve. She was able to counter this passive resistance only with feelings of helpless rage or equally helpless tears.

"You're a shit!" she said angrily.

He took that as grounds to walk out of the apartment.

Whereas you can probably see why Ruth (in the first example) loses, it is less obvious with Edith. At first glance, nothing in this example has anything to do with smiling or submission. Nevertheless, both stories have the same roots. Neither of the women really believes she has any influence in getting her husband to share in doing the family chores. These, too, are forms of passive surrender and part of the Mona Lisa trap. Edith does not think she has the right to demand Bruce's help, and it makes her furious. Somehow she senses that something is going wrong because after seeing his tired expression, she has unexpectedly fallen into the sympathetic *understanding trap.* A little voice tells her, "You can't expect that of him; he's all done in." She shows less understanding for her own fatigue.

Imagine yourself saying, "I can understand that you're tired, but still I expect you to . . ." Allow yourself to demand something from other people.

On the other hand, Pauline's *successful* attempt demonstrates the kind of mentality that can protect you from the Mona Lisa trap. She and John, her friend, have been living together for eight months in an apartment they rent jointly. Pauline's basic motto is:

Don't Be Afraid of Clear or Tough Confrontations.

With this attitude she got John to do his share of the housecleaning they both hate. Pauline pursued her objective clearly and unambiguously; she knew exactly what she wanted. While they were sitting in the living room just talking amiably, she asked him almost incidentally, "Hey, John, when are you going to clean the bathroom?"

He looked at her in amazement. "I've never cleaned the bathroom!"

"Right! And I want that to change," Pauline said.

"No way!" John declared emphatically.

Pauline was unmoved. "I've been annoyed with you for months because you've been avoiding this chore. I won't put up with it anymore. Either we find a solution together, or we're going to have a serious discussion about our relationship. And neither one of us knows how that's going to turn out."

Thus they had quickly arrived at a critical point. Pauline had given it a lot of thought. She knew that she would not be able to put up with playing the maid permanently. In the end it would all turn on the same question anyway. John felt he was being blackmailed, and he was. But Pauline knew that if she gave in on this point, she might just as well move out immediately. She sat facing John. She was ticked off and was not going to swerve from her position. John sensed that. He looked at her thoughtfully; he knew she was right. Still he tried to break down her resolve.

First, he flattered her, "You're much better at it."

Then he threatened her. "If both of us are responsible for everything, then it will all end in chaos."

Next, he tried to cast doubt on their relationship. "I think that your feelings for me have changed radically."

He tried being gentle. Then he yelled at her.

Pauline stuck to her guns. "You're going to clean the bathroom" was her clear and unyielding demand. She met his various attempts to change her mind with serious, angry, or amused responses. But her decision was *irreversible.* Either he was going to stop ducking the housework, or their relationship was finished.

Many women shy away from facing up to such a dire alternative. They can't imagine jeopardizing their relationship, and so they fall victim to every form of blackmail, either direct or indirect, that threatens to put an end to it. At this point most women would probably say, "Would I jeopardize my relationship for such a petty thing?" And they'd look skeptical and incredulous. But unfortunately that's how it is. It's the supposed trifles, which by themselves seem ridiculous, that let women slip little by little into the role of the loser. It's the little things partners demand of each other that matter. Women often think it's the total number of submissions that counts. But it is precisely these individual, little, seemingly innocuous favors that make a woman the underdog.

Did you blanch on reading this section? Or did it make you feel a little queasy? Perhaps you didn't want to know all the details of what's involved in getting out of the Mona Lisa trap. Indeed, the challenge is radical. In the final analysis, you'll always be left on the sidelines as long as you're willing to patiently adapt.

If you don't pursue your own interests directly, if you accept detours, if you avoid honest confrontation, and if you shrink from inescapable conclusions, you won't be able to build up your self-confidence. Rather, by your actions, you'll be torpedoing your own emancipation.

If you want to get out of the role of the despondent, compliant woman with a smile, you have to fight honestly and openly for your own interests and be willing to stand by them. Moreover, you have to get out of a relationship if many fundamentally important *little things* are continually settled to your disadvantage.

This won't make you into an ornery battle-ax, but into an independent human being.

Escaping the Mona Lisa smile will make your life more intense, more independent, more spontaneous, and less predictable and sheltered; although your existence may be less calm, it will definitely be less bland, dependent, and artificial.

If women want to take equal rights seriously, then they must accept the fact that only an independent woman can be entitled to those rights. There is no such thing as being a "little bit" entitled to equality, just as you can't be a little bit pregnant.

The woman who thinks she can be more secure by waiving equal rights is going to have a rude awakening. For she, too, can be deserted, deceived, and humiliated. If she's ensnared in the Mona Lisa trap, she'll wake up in a pitiful state—without a job or professional training and no money of her own. All her life she was the *good* wife; she put up with a lot and continued to hope. And at the bitter end she's going to be shaken to the marrow by so much injustice. After all, she always did everything for everybody, making all kinds of sacrifices, even in bed.

All for nothing. It will be a painful awakening.

You say that can't happen to you? You've got a firm hold on your husband? He turns over his paycheck to you? He adores you? Maybe. But can you stand *him?* Haven't you had it "up to here"? Don't you secretly long for a partner with whom you could pick a quarrel once in a while? If not, you're a rare exception.

The Relationship Traps

Here are five:

The Understanding Trap
The Helper Trap
The Victim Trap
The Modesty Trap
The Pity Trap

There are many forms of female submission. Giving a name to your own pattern can often be the first step to liberation. I'm going to describe some dramatic cases that illustrate where harmless beginnings can lead when women won't change self-damaging behaviors. At the same time I hope to sharpen your perception of these traps. Vigilance is essential, for every woman is going to be tempted at some time or other to give up her own positions on various issues with a smile.

The Understanding Trap

Here the leitmotif is "I have to be understanding (read, sympathetic) of my partner's emotional and psychological problems."

You say without thinking, "Oh, I understand" or "I understand the problem." You tolerate somebody's late arrival; you "understand" when someone is treated unjustly. Women have understanding or sympathy for many things; they often comment gently or understandingly on outrageous and inconsiderate behavior even when they have to bear the brunt of it.

They tolerate intolerable behavior. With an understanding smile they put up with behavior that definitely ought to be condemned and for which an apology is clearly in order. A woman who's been insulted will "understand" the cad who made the uncalled-for or insolent remarks. For instance, in the course of a conversation with friends, a husband disparages the intellectual capacity of his wife. "My sweetie," he laughs, "doesn't get it." But instead of taking a definite stand and paying him back in his own coin, *she* merely smiles. Rarely do we become aware of the implications of this kind of behavior.

Do you show false understanding or sympathy?
As soon as you use the word "understand," ask yourself:
What is it that I understand?
Why do I understand it?
How deep is my understanding?
How much do I really agree with the situation that I'm claiming to understand?

For example, do you really understand when your girlfriend tells you, shortly before she's supposed to meet you, that she can't go to the concert with you because her husband will be angry, lonely, or suspicious? Women often equate the knowledge that they can't change another person with "being understanding." Naturally this doesn't have much to do with real *understanding.* And even if you comprehend his motives, that is no reason to let him walk all over you.

Originally, *to understand* meant that you could comprehend a connection, a technical or logical construct. Thus one could *understand* the conflict between capital and labor, or how to solve a quadratic equation. At the same time understanding reflects one's readiness to comprehend emotional ramifications. You understand someone mourning for a dead person, a friend's heartache, or the anger of someone who's been emotionally hurt. On top of that the word has acquired the connotation of superficial tolerance. Unfortunately, it's the secondary meanings that are being used more and more. Today *understand* often means: *to overlook, ignore, not to intervene.* Yet it is quite possible to understand and still disapprove.

Often you put up with the way a person acts only because you don't have the courage to disapprove openly. And that is how the original meaning—*to understand* logically or acoustically—has gradually changed into a synonym for putting up with a way of acting that in itself one disapproves of, despises, or even condemns.

We also use the word *understand* in a certain polite-pedagogical context. It's become a social convention. You use the word *understand* when you want to express disapproval of a particular behavior and hope that in the future the criticized behavior will change. You say, "I understand," and it's just an empty phrase. For whatever reason, you want to spare the person you're criticizing a more direct correction or reprimand. You think your expression and tone of voice show enough disapproval. Your words express thoughtfulness and courtesy toward the person being criticized. One certainly can't object to that, and in many situations that is how the word *understand* is used.

What is important is to be sure that everybody involved deciphers the nuances and differences in your verbal and nonverbal messages the same way.

All too often, however, the word *understand* is not used in this polite sense, but rather to hush up something, to absolve someone of guilt. Inexcusable behavior—without any further examination—is thus blamed *not* on the culprit but on an outside cause. Eventually the individual being criticized is relieved of personal accountability through *understanding.*

Even crude misbehavior, such as insolence or aggressiveness, is considered an unfortunate consequence of poor upbringing or explained away as inevitable, and *it is understood.* Unfortunately, nowadays we frequently read or hear about extreme examples of violence and show a lot of "understanding." A thirty-year-old teacher explained to me, "The fellows who did this are unemployed; they have no job prospects. They've been stirred up. In a way, you can understand their anger." His attempt to relativize the situation by the use of "in a way" misses the point. The dangerous pattern of solving (suppressing) one's problems by violence against others is interpreted as an inevitable result of social circumstances. Nobody demands real accountability anymore from the roughnecks or their spiritual accomplices.

Understanding at Any Price?
Understanding is an ambivalent, contradictory concept. The Mona Lisa "understanding" trap can be better recognized if we examine it more critically. If you *understand* why your boss is in a bad mood, you may already have fallen into the understanding trap. If you *understand* and sympathize with your moody husband, then you're definitely caught in the understanding trap.

Often it's hard for women to be aware of the little everyday versions of this trap, which has many faces. It has been drummed into women and girls that to *understand others* is a great virtue and highly desirable behavior. Having understanding for the weaknesses of others has almost become a symbol of feminine virtue— even when these weaknesses are tantamount to a slap in the face.

We try to teach children, especially girls, that this kind of *understanding* is an expression of humaneness. I've never quite understood the connection because it seems to me that from the time they were little, women were being taught to put up with something that was bad and to indirectly call it good. Instead they should have learned to say clearly and definitely, "I didn't like that" or "I thought that was mean" or "That was really a shitty thing to do!" And so understanding gets to have the same meaning as excusing, putting up with, or enduring something good-naturedly.

Understanding turns into a personal trap when you understand behavior that is directed against you. As long as you're not directly affected by someone's behavior, it's lack of personal courage or fear of confrontation that keeps you from calling a spade a spade and taking a definite stand against it. But understanding becomes self-destructive when you patiently put up with nastiness, intrigues, or in extreme cases, even violence directed against you. The consequences include constant depression, deep-seated anxieties, feelings of inferiority, and even psychological and physical illnesses. Once women enter the cycle of self-surrender, they often descend inexorably into a vortex of despair and complete helplessness.

Physical violence is seldom involved in the understanding trap. If it ever does become a factor, then it's only after long years of patient understanding. Therefore, initially a woman will hardly ever realize the danger she's getting into. For one thing, it is "in" today to be understanding. (The word *liberal* is often applied in this sense of excessive forbearance or tolerance). For another, we are demonstrating our human sympathy or empathy when we *understand something.* This is a value that almost all women accept. One likes to believe that one has empathy for others. You recognize it in sentences such as "I'm a good listener" or "I'm good at sensing how others feel or putting myself in their shoes." But what this often means is that ways of acting or thinking are uncritically accepted, even when they harm a third person.

No sooner does the forbearing woman resign herself than the understanding trap snaps shut. At that point she capitulates to her tormentor with the implied message: "I surrender. I won't resist your hurting me anymore." If she can find no way out of this surrender, then unpleasant dramatic developments are unavoidable. Everyone knows some woman who continues to live in an absolutely ruinous relationship and doesn't dare make an attempt to break out. She'll stick it out to the bitter end.

The way leading into this trap can look quite harmless. Hilda, a lawyer, married Stephen, also a lawyer who had his own law office. Her dreams soared. They would have a joint office, each with his own large room, they would discuss legal problems, and thoroughly enjoy the little leisure time they'd have. But what happened was quite different. Stephen refused to let Hilda appear in court; he thought she lacked the required personality and persuasiveness. So Hilda was left to pore over legal commentary. She actually was better at that than he was; she had done distinctly better on her written exams in law school and had also passed her orals brilliantly. Yet Hilda understood and forgave. Stephen wanted to make a name for himself, and so this division of labor was very convenient for him. She put together airtight, unassailable legal arguments, and he presented them in court. The laurels, he kept for himself.

He also left the management of the office to Hilda. She wrote the briefs, handled the invoices, and took care of his appointments. In the meantime he made contacts with clients, which really meant sitting in a café and reading the morning paper. Their friends all knew what was going on, even Hilda. But she "understood." It certainly was a mistake on her part to play second fiddle this way, but it didn't get really bad until Stephen began to make snide remarks about her office work. Suddenly it was as though that was the only thing she was good for, as though it had been a generous act on his part to let her work for him. None of the clients knew Hilda; they insisted on being represented by Stephen since they had no idea of what went on in the office. Almost no one knew that she was also a lawyer. In the end Hilda was all at sea. The distortion of her role worried her a lot. Mistakes crept into her work; she became increasingly distraught but didn't dare say anything against Stephen. Finally one day she came to her senses when he slapped her because there were misspellings in her typing; she packed her bags. Today she is divorced from Stephen and has become a junior partner in a well-known law office.

In Hilda's case it was clear to all her friends that her *understanding* was a bad mistake. And there's no doubt that talking with friends helped her to make a successful break—albeit a little late.

Unfortunately, the understanding trap closes even in less destructive situations. As soon as a woman accepts the fact that a man who blows his top, who rants and raves, won't in any way apologize for this behavior, the trap snaps shut.

Very important: Blowing one's top by itself is not the deciding factor; any person can fly off the handle once in a while. It's only when his partner is willing to skip a sincere apology that it becomes a problem.

Lip service does not adequately compensate for gruff behavior. **Did you ever have to apologize for blowing your stack? That's a good sign; you won't stumble into the Mona Lisa trap too easily.**

Someone who is proud of always being able to control her temper is perhaps overlooking her fear of the consequences that flying off the handle might have. It's no disgrace to rant and rave once in a while. But you have to be able to apologize. And generally the problem was that you merely used the wrong tone of voice; the *essence* of what you said should rarely be taken back.

An apology for gruff behavior does not have to be made verbally or even formally, but it must be clear that there was an apology, and it must be accepted as such by both parties to the argument. It won't help *you* to accept the bouquet of flowers he brings as an apology if he sees it more like a settlement of damages for injuries inflicted. That would be like being paid off with flowers for silently putting up with things—a bad deal.

An externally harmless but internally dangerous form of the understanding trap appears in relationships in which, on the surface, there seem to be hardly any serious differences between the partners. But in such a relationship of mutual arrangements you see subliminal hostility exposed when one of the partners unexpectedly forgets himself. Usually that happens after too much alcohol, stress at work, too little sleep, differences about the children, or rows with parents or in-laws. Seemingly out of the blue, an abyss opens up. At a moment like this people show their deeply rooted and usually well-concealed mutual hatred. If you have had such experiences and know that in some situations you've been attacked boorishly, humiliatingly, or gruffly, and that afterwards there was no real apology to show that the other person was truly sorry about what slipped out, then you are not faced with just a onetime gaffe, but you're caught in the understanding trap. All warning signals should be flashing red when you hear yourself saying things like, "That's just the way he is"; "He can't help it"; "He doesn't mean it"; "When he's had too much to drink, he's not himself"; "Yes, but his heart's in the right place."

When a woman looks for reasons that would make inexcusable behavior excusable, or that would explain it, she is already caught in the Mona Lisa trap. It's even worse if she sees no way out of this silent toleration. The dead-end situation is aggravated because the victim of such attacks is sending a message to her oppressor that she would never put into so many words, namely: "I deserve it; my misery and the way you're treating me are my fault." And so he is getting indirect justification for his behavior. It becomes increasingly easier for him to attack his victim and to hurt her psychologically or even physically. And all the time he's doing it, he'll be telling himself he is right because his victim unintentionally justifies his oppressive behavior.

In the understanding trap, physical attacks occur rarely, and if so, usually during a quarrel. Psychological attacks predominate, with the injured partner holding out and hoping for a change in her attacker's attitude. Physical violence is more likely to be associated with the victim trap.

The Helper Trap

The leitmotif is "If I help him/her, I'll get his/her attention and devotion."

The helper trap is in most cases an escalation of the understanding trap in which misunderstood altruistic motives come into play. The helper wants to lead those who have gone astray back onto the right path, to protect them from the threat of an apparent or real disaster, or save them from some unhappy situation they brought upon themselves.

A special aspect of the helper trap is the helper's potential for aggressiveness, which can be considerable. *Helpers* can dump frustration and reproaches on their *wards*. They may dramatically underscore all his or her misery; sometimes they even enjoy explaining just how he or she came to be in this dire situation. While they're telling the story they may put on a sad, concerned expression, yet often it's accompanied by a gentle or even triumphant smile.

But there is one thing that helpers never do; they never write *finis*. And they won't let the one who's gone astray really get back on his feet; he won't achieve that goal. The helper is a building block in his system, but she steadfastly refuses to recognize that. She helps him uphold his system; she tolerates or, even worse, misuses her erring charge to bolster her own feeling of self-worth. That is why she supports him, more or less. She can read him the riot act in very reproachful tones (usually alternating this with expressions of devotion), but what she's really saying is: "I'm putting up with you and your harmful behavior."

The spouses or partners of alcoholics offer a classic example of this trap. Alcoholism is an extremely serious psychic sickness, and I certainly don't want to put all relatives of people who have an addiction into a bad light. But relatives often put up with an alcoholic's insidious self-destruction. This is especially so when it comes to a person who drinks all the time but consumes just enough to stay overtly sober because he doesn't want to be labeled a problem drinker—and usually isn't identified as an alcoholic. They tolerate or support him by offering various alibis. They deny the real dimension of his addiction when they talk to him, his doctors, close relatives, and often to themselves. The alcoholic would not be an addict if he did not gratefully accept such help and use it to convince himself that he doesn't really have a serious problem.

We are interested here in the motives of the helper. What does she gain from this sort of denial? Her social gain is obvious; after all, who really likes to admit that a family member is an addict? It is even harder to acknowledge that one's own husband has such problems. This is the point at which the Mona Lisa syndrome begins, because the majority of helpers feel powerless and at the mercy of the alcoholic. Hardly anyone knows how to deal meaningfully with the lies, manipulation, and repeated promises or half-hearted attempts by alcoholics to "go on the wagon." Wanting to help becomes a self-deceiving lie. The fear of actively confronting and dealing with the problem conceals the fear of unpleasant consequences. The helper smiles her helpless smile because she knows that she herself ought to be looking for help that might give her the courage to do something.

Common Helper Traps
Naturally the helper syndrome also comes in less serious forms: An imperceptible helper trap springs shut when people want to put another person back on the right path, not realizing that they themselves draw a hidden benefit from his abnormal behavior. They can feel secretly superior and enjoy their victim's dependency on them. Less harmful versions of this are the partners of smokers, of people who are overweight, or those with neurotic anxieties. At least as seen from the outside, the helpers have these problems in hand and are tolerant toward their spouses' minor addictions. Also in this group is the wife of a "mama's boy" who is trying to free him from his mother's apron strings and who wants to construct new but equally disadvantageous ties to her husband.

Activists and Homebodies (Fledglings Who Don't Want to Leave the Nest)
On another level of the helper trap we often find the wife of an intrepid mountain climber, a dedicated athlete, or an inveterate globe-trotter. In order to give HIM the chance for total self-realization, she puts aside her own aims in life. Again and again, as the caring helper, she tolerates, supports, and compensates for her spouse's attempts to escape.

But the helper trap also closes on a helper whose husband is afraid of life, or who withdraws from society and people. This, too, is a rewarding area where she can sacrifice herself: Day in and dreary day out the helper consoles or quarrels with her husband who is running away from life. For these frightened partners, the wife takes on the mother role. Like a mother, the helper-wife does everything possible to remove the obstacles that these anxieties create.

Neither provides any real change.

Two examples:

The badminton player. His whole life was taken up with the game. He went to badminton matches, he played on his club's varsity team. To stay in shape he went cross-country running; twice a week he trained at his club; and one evening a week he gave lessons. Whenever he met other people, all conversation revolved around the sport—the latest sneakers, the newest shuttlecocks, rackets, stringing, the other players, the standings on the charts, etc. Nobody had a chance to talk about anything else. Unfortunately, his wife had little genuine interest in sports. But for *his* sake she concentrated on making his playing—which meant everything to him— possible. She did not ask him to help with the housework, or to spend time with her, or to have her *own* needs satisfied; she "was happy when he was happy." Perhaps she was proud of him; perhaps she got vicarious satisfaction from his commitment, his total involvement in his hobby. It was never clear. She only sat there, smiling gently. She saw to his meals, his drinks, his clean laundry. As far as I could see, she had no apparent interests of her own.

The gardener. He spent almost all of his leisure time in his greenhouse. He earned good money, and they owned a large house with a truly remarkable greenhouse and a garden that was just as impressive. His wife enjoyed this perfection. It was really a feast for the eyes. But she had absolutely no interest in plants. And so she withdrew; she read novels or, armed with a long list he had given her, she went shopping for garden tools and equipment. He felt it was too much of a bother to deal with salespeople, to order things, to inquire about certain items, and to do all that driving to the stores. Her stock phrase was: "He needs these things and I like to help him." She loved the theater, but she couldn't get him to go with her more than once a year. She didn't want to go without him, and she surely couldn't let him sit home alone. Friends rarely came to their house; true, he liked to show off his magnificent garden and talk about it, but nobody was encouraged to stay very long. He thought there was something not quite right with simply sitting down and chatting with other people. He easily got bored and didn't know what to say. *She* had no real interests of her own, and only wanted to make it possible for him to be *completely absorbed with his hobby.*

The two stories belong together; both women have internalized their self-abnegation to such an extent that all conflict with their husbands has been eliminated or avoided.

The Victim Trap

The leitmotif is "It is my destiny to sacrifice myself for the happiness of others."

Several years ago psychologists tried to find out why some people are more often the victims of crimes than others. But it was difficult to objectively examine the degree to which a victim participated in the crime committed against him. The investigators were reproached for turning the victims into accomplices. It was hard to accept the idea of a victim's complicity. The criminals ought to bear the entire responsibility. The discussion went right past the specific subject of the research: whether women should stop wearing miniskirts or use less makeup because they might be attracting criminal behavior. The discussion was limited to a minor aspect of victim research (victimology). In essence, the investigators discovered that these external factors (the miniskirts and makeup) were not typical for victims of multiple crimes. Actually, it was quite the opposite. The women whose pocketbooks were repeatedly snatched (by coincidence?), or who were raped more than once, were unprepossessing, shy, and fearful.

It isn't easy for a rape or crime victim to accept that she herself is somehow responsible for what happened. Yet, sad to say, it is also typical that people who tend to be victimized feel guilty, intimidated, and helpless when these connections are pointed out to them. One might say that people become victims of violence more often when something in their appearance and gestures communicates fear and defenselessness, even giving the impression that they *expect* something of this sort is going to happen to them.

Helen, a thirty-four-year-old buyer, said, "I know what that's like. It's happened to me. In my office they suspect me of misusing and ruining an expensive label-addressing machine. Or people accuse me of starting rumors in my neighborhood even though I try to stay out of things as much as possible. My husband claims I'm responsible for the crises in our marriage. And what really has me worried is that I can't stop thinking there might be some truth to all the things they're saying."

Other women said they felt guilty for their children's bad behavior, or the lack of a husband's sexual interest, or the loss of a job. They always feel *they* are somehow to blame. Sobbing, Helen told me about her problems, how bad she felt, and how she attracted accusations as if by magic. She seldom found a way to refute these false charges. At work she really believed she had done something wrong while operating the machine, even though there were no objective reasons to think so. After a family argument she remembered the critical thoughts she had had about one of her uncles. She rooted around for arguments that could lay the blame on her. Consistently she herself delivers the ammunition to her opponents. It is hardly surprising that when she was involved in a no-fault automobile accident, it took a lawyer to prove her innocence. She had entangled herself in a web of self-recriminations. Lack of self-esteem and constant guilt feelings attract bad luck—as if by magic.

Should You Make Sacrifices for Others?

Women who tend to be victims often have another self-destructive habit. They think they can atone for their victim role by behaving like saints. A woman will do everything she can for her relatives, her husband, her boss, and office colleagues, and receive no thanks at all for it. No matter how much she sacrifices for others, they just take it all for granted. Nor was there any reason that they should have felt guilty, because nobody had asked her to make these sacrifices, to constantly give her all. She alone took care of a sick aunt; she was the only one in the office to put in overtime every evening without complaining; she was the one who took the family car to be repaired even though her husband and grown son had nothing better to do than sit at home in front of the TV or while away their time some other way.

It isn't easy for the self-sacrificing woman to do all this. She's often ill. She suffers under this self-inflicted burden and yet continues without complaining. At most, her face may reveal the great effort or strain it is costing her. If she notices someone looking at her, she quickly forces a smile to her lips, no matter what it takes.

It's highly likely that her own suffering is her goal.

Her pain becomes a guarantee for her happiness and the goodwill of others toward her. And that is what the sacrificing woman lives for, so that others may have a good life.

Our model of the ideal mother incorporates many of these traits: The most important thing is for her family to be well and for the children to be happy so that nobody can say anything bad about the family. This mind-set has many masochistic aspects. These women have made a pact with the devil; they hope to buy the happiness of their families with their own suffering. In spite of that, their goal is often unclear; the only discernible pattern is: "I have to make the ultimate effort, to make sacrifices, to deny myself, and to do without." Sometimes I think these women no longer know for whom they're actually making all these sacrifices. Self-sacrifice has become an end in itself. For them, a self-contained cycle has started; the purpose of life is to suffer. This view is often associated with a fatalistic resignation to one's destiny or devotion to God. Yet there is no genuine piousness behind such an attitude, for it is in a hidden way also a challenge. In the chapter about learned helplessness I described in some detail the childhood experiences that typically lead to the Mona Lisa traps. Learned helplessness is a significant feature of the victim trap.

Frequently such women are in a relationship with a partner who takes it for granted that sacrifices should be made for him—a partner who basks in his wife's or companion's unconditional devotion. Women who are the victims of male violence also belong in this group. They know that they'll continue to be abused within their relationships, and yet can't manage to get out.

Here are two examples to help you identify the self-sacrifice trap:

Emma was married to an irascible, bad-tempered, and probably psychologically disturbed man. He was not physically abusive toward her, but he would complain at the top of his voice—two to three hours at a time without a pause—going on about the world, their relationship, and his bad luck. Most of the time he would adopt a monotonous aggressive singsong tone that would sporadically explode into outbursts of rage. During these tirades he always made sure that his wife heard him; he followed her from room to room, rambling on and on. If she answered in any way, he would raise his voice and make gruff gestures. It often went on several hours until, exhausted, he would fall into bed and drop off to sleep. Emma assumed this sort of behavior was relatively normal; it never occurred to her to ask anyone whether it was. Nor did she ask herself whether she wanted to continue to endure this torture—and that's what it really was for her. "After all, he's my husband," she answered if anyone expressed any doubts about her patient tolerance.

Another example. A young woman handed over her entire inheritance to her husband so he could start a computer store. Even though she knew very well that his ideas about making a fast buck

("Once it's on track, all I'll have to do is go in to pick up the day's take") were completely unrealistic, she was unable to say "no" to him. He'd never done well at his job, and couldn't get along with either his bosses or his co-workers. He easily became aggressive and reacted with verbal abuse if something rubbed him the wrong way. On top of that, his paycheck never seemed to be enough. Now he saw his big chance. *She* thought she couldn't deprive him of the opportunity even though she had a bad feeling about it. Deep down, she knew that it wouldn't work. Eventually her entire inheritance went down the drain. She was glad, at least, that there wasn't a mountain of debts to be paid.

More Moderate Forms of Self-Sacrifice

Do you think these last two examples are the sad outgrowths of excessive readiness to sacrifice oneself? They are indeed. But they're not unique; I meet up with the phenomenon of self-sacrifice every day.

For instance, there's the twenty-two-year-old woman who doesn't want to desert her friend even though he's plundered her savings account. And the helpful thirty-eight-year-old wife who takes her husband's shaving gear over to his lover's apartment. There's the twenty-nine-year-old wife who has her wages transferred to her unemployed husband's bank account because he has debts. The grandmother who regularly hands over a third of her Social Security check to her sons and daughters. She herself stays at home in a cold room in order to be able to make these generous gestures, yet her children rarely come to see her. There is the married woman who sends her husband on a trip to Europe by himself because he works so hard all year, and there isn't enough money for *both* of them to go. There is the wife who puts up with a husband who buys expensive motorcycles even though the car she drives to work is old and breaks down all the time.

Other examples of self-sacrifice: the woman who goes with her husband to see one film after another, none being of the slightest interest to her; the woman who puts up with her husband spending a third of the family income on his hobby; the woman who takes on housecleaning work in addition to her regular job because her husband has run up gambling debts; and the woman who forgives her husband for the night that swallowed up a thousand bucks. He was with the guys, he said. She never found out where.

There are many other examples, and often I hear extremely indulgent excuses. "It really isn't that bad." "Men need that sort of thing." "That's just the way he is. I can't change him. Should I leave him just because of that?" These are all instances of helpless self-sacrifice, declining to exert influence, playing the victim.

Strikingly characteristic of this sort of self-sacrifice is some women's headlong rush to make things easy for everybody else without even waiting to be asked—anticipating what the other person wants, needs, or would find pleasant. Modestly and inconspicuously they use the "insightfulness" they have acquired. They sacrifice and deny themselves as though there were no higher good.

The Modesty Trap

The leitmotif is "It is a true virtue to put one's own demands and interests last."

There's an old saying: Modesty may be a virtue, but you can get further without it.

Ironically, immodesty is often approved in men with a wink or a slap on the back. But for women, modesty is the essential virtue. Selflessness is the mark of perfect femininity.

Women are modest for many reasons—such as lack of self-confidence, expectation of heavenly or earthly rewards, fear of conflicts, and last but not least, hope for protection and respect.

The modesty of these women hides doubts about their own practical competence and their ability to cope with life. With deferential, disguised submission, they hope to be better protected from attacks or criticism from their colleagues and husbands or partners.

Here are a few examples of false or misplaced modesty:

Nicole was living with an older man. For various reasons, they could not and did not want to get married. He pressed her repeatedly to take out an insurance policy on his life so that she would at least have some financial security in case he died. There would also be major advantages if *she* were to take out the policy because then there would be no inheritance tax. He was a tax adviser and knew what he was talking about. Naturally *he* would pay the premiums. He asked her repeatedly to buy such an insurance policy. Nicole was touched that he cared so much, but she didn't want to accept his gift. It is hardly surprising that she smiled charmingly as she rejected his suggestion. It was too much, she said; she wanted only to live happily with him. She could not accept this "provision" for her future.

I probably would not have remembered this episode if their love affair had not had such a tragic end. Unexpectedly, he had a stroke and died. She had to move out of their apartment, and although she was distraught with grief, she had no choice but to go back to work four weeks later. "If I had been able to take half a year off," she said, "I could have taken my final leave from him the way we always imagined, and come to terms with my grief. But there was no money for that. I should have accepted his suggestion. Then I could have used the money to take the six months off."

False Modesty

The example of Eleni is less dramatic. She was employed in a nursing home for the elderly and liked her work. She was a good organizer and got along well with colleagues and patients. The management offered her a promotion to ward supervisor. Eleni asked for time to think it over and then rejected the offer. An older colleague had applied for the job, and Eleni knew that if she declined, he would get it. She thought it wouldn't be right for him to be passed over. Smilingly she told me of her refined sense of justice. I considered it false modesty. Nearly all promotions mean that another person—whether you know him or not—will miss out on getting a job.

Another example. Rachel's three-month maternity leave is just about over, but her firm refuses to hold her job for her. If she doesn't return within the prescribed period, she was told, they'll hire someone else. Her husband understood her dilemma. After some hesitation, he offered to take paternity leave. It wouldn't be easy for him; he was afraid of being teased by his co-workers, but it was also a sort of challenge for him. He had a civil service job, and his application for leave was sure to be granted. But Rachel hesitated; she didn't want him to make sacrifices. After a long back and forth, she told her employer she would not return to work before the deadline. She would rather face the fact that she wouldn't be able to get her old job back than accept her husband's offer. "I can't ask him to do that. He won't be able to put up with the teasing he'd get while spending the entire day at home, or sitting around with all those women in the toddler play group."

These were merely excuses. Her husband had made the decision to do it long ago.

Rachel also is a victim of her modesty. Deep down she couldn't bear the idea that for her sake her husband would be the butt of sly looks and spiteful remarks, just because she wanted to go back to her old job. She enjoyed her work and would have been glad to get back to her desk. Her false modesty made her come to a dubious decision.

False modesty occurs less frequently within relationships, although you can find it there too. Mostly, however, it appears at the workplace in dealings with colleagues, friends, or acquaintances. It sneaks in unexpectedly. High praise for a piece of independent work is played down. You credit your own achievements to coincidence and help from others—all accompanied by a sweet, coy smile. The working woman who postpones changing to a job that would open up a new and interesting field to her because her boss "needs" her is caught in the trap—in fact, she's in a dual trap. The *modest helper,* that's a real double mistake.

One woman, who climbed out of the trap, was convinced that "the worst thing about the modesty trap is your unspoken self-appraisal as being too stupid and therefore not having the right to make any demands."

There's a lot of truth in that. Even though modest women might try to talk us into believing that they followed a higher goal in their lives, I had the impression that in each case self-doubt was the major motivating force behind their self-denial—no matter what sublime and honorable motives they tried to talk themselves into.

There is strong reason to believe that modesty is socially transmitted. Often mothers and daughters both suffer from the symptom of false self-denial or self-sacrifice. This game can get quite bizarre when they unintentionally enter a contest for top honors in modesty. It may be quite polite and seemingly friendly, but behind the modest facade there is a tough struggle going on about who can be the most modest, who will be allowed to make the sacrifice. At that point the knowing spectator is overcome by a secret joy; for often it becomes apparent that in a real battle of modesty against modesty, woman against woman (rarely man against man), an undreamed-of fighting spirit that would otherwise have remained well concealed comes to the fore.

I once heard such a pair, mother and daughter, whispering together about who should get a valuable silver vase that belonged to an aunt who had died. "It will look better in your apartment." "But you'll be able to enjoy it longer." "You spent much more time with her." "You were her favorite niece." "Please, you take it." "No, I can't take it, under any circumstances." In the end, a distant relative took the vase, saying, "If you two can't get your act together . . ."

Modesty is socialized through role models, but also by way of parental rewards for modest behavior. Loving, strong parents, especially, manage to raise overmodest children. Modesty is the approach these children use to submit to their parents. Such parents give their children little breathing room. They have exact ideas of what their children are supposed to be when they grow up.

The Pity Trap

The leitmotif is "My commiseration will make your pain go away."

Being able to feel sympathy for others is important. In relationships, however, sympathy cannot replace love. Sympathy and love don't fit well together.

When it is pronounced, the sympathy trap is relatively easy to recognize. Everybody can see right away that a woman is tying herself to a partner out of sympathy if he has obvious problems in coping with life. She may look after a weak husband who is pushed around at work, or she may protect a man who (as the younger brother) never stepped out of his bigger brother's shadow. She'll console a man who admired his strong father, but was helpless when it came to following in his footsteps. She pampers him because he will never be able to outgrow the role of the fearful son or, worse yet, the son who is a failure. She doesn't love him. If he weren't so pitiful, she would have left him long ago.

The Disastrous Consequences

It is difficult to recognize harmful sympathy when the suffering of the pitied person (e.g., self-doubt, depression, loss of a job) is only expressed within an intimate circle and doesn't reach the outside world. Here you meet seemingly happy, intact families who suddenly are overwhelmed by disaster. How do these catastrophes happen?

Sympathizers often have the harmful effect of not being of any real help, but instead only adding to the problem. A husband loses his job, but his wife maintains a facade to the outside world. This is often the only help she, a sympathizer, gives. She offers him no opportunity to let off steam or to unburden himself, nor does she offer any relief or support. Apparently unforseeable family tragedies sometimes have such histories. A brief newspaper headline ("Man

Shoots Wife and Child") reports the tragic ending. If you know the background, some of these crazy acts can at least be explained in part:

An already weak husband loses the last bit of stability. The only "solution" left to him, because he cannot admit his weakness, is to free *all* of them, his wife and child, from this miserable life.

Many relationships are stabilized by a seesaw mechanism. If one partner is feeling down, then the other is up and can be supportive. However, this reciprocity didn't work in the cases mentioned above.

What effect does sympathy have on the one who is suffering?

This question is a surefire means of distinguishing genuine from false sympathy. Genuine sympathy that is based on a strong self-confident attitude usually relieves and calms the sufferer. Often it enables him to take some steps toward a potential solution, but at the least he can get some measure of release and peace and see things in perspective.

False sympathy has a completely different effect. It is a well-concealed attempt to overcome, by means of hypocritical compassion, your own fear that the one who is suffering will fail. Your theme might be: I feel sorry for you; please be strong again, or at least take away my fear of your weakness.

But there is another aspect to this. People who suffered in their childhood—whether from violence, excessive demands made on them, lack of love, or loneliness—frequently develop a tendency to symbolically inflict on their fellow human beings or animals the deprivation they themselves suffered. Sad to say, some animal protectionists, no matter how correct their basic position is, have to be put into this category. Often you can sense concealed aggression in these activists, a reflection of the pain they themselves suffered.

Once they have directed their sympathy toward another person and so achieved a symbolic liberation from their early experiences, a vicious circle is initiated. The sympathy misfires—at least in the long run. The sympathizer experiences a disappointment that weighs on her mind because her attempt to help has failed. And so she unintentionally is forced into the role of the person who once made her suffer: Nobody helped her then, and now she senses her own inability to help someone else. She is just as bad as those people who surrounded her in her childhood and who refused to help her.

Compassion is often related to a visual experience. For example, if people could not see pictures of misery and suffering on television, their sympathy—expressed in their readiness to contribute money to various causes—would certainly not be as great.

But the positive meaning of the word does not apply to this kind of sympathy. Serious and meaningful sympathy flows from a different source. Our compassion is aroused because we feel a sincere, warm connection to someone. We empathize with him or suffer with him even without any visual presentation of his plight.

In the case of false sympathy, the sympathizer makes little or no claim that he can or ought to help the other person out of his trouble or suffering. Therefore, this form of sympathy is usually coupled with helpless activism that is more likely to worry or disquiet the "victim" than to calm him. Often the sympathizer, rather than the actual sufferer, is more likely to dissolve in tears. The sympathizer always pities herself, too; she suffers twice. Yet the sympathizer wants to keep her composure, which usually means a distorted smile. Most of the time, behind it all, she feels she doesn't want to lose her self-control, start to cry, and look unattractive. A fateful Sword of Damocles hangs over the sympathizer: the worry that she herself is arousing sympathy. This may be one of the most threatening ideas, even though the desire to be pitied is very deep rooted. Occasionally it surfaces violently, only to be vigorously suppressed a little later.

Chapter 9

The
Docile
Woman

.

Women Need Comrades-in-Arms

Women must look for help and moral support from other women who really want to change things. But they should be aware that often even women who are close friends would rather leave things as they are, although they may say just the opposite.

A rebellious woman who turns her back on the old clichés may get the reputation of being a she-devil, a battle-ax, or worse. But she shouldn't let that bother her. In her efforts "to do it *her* way," to change traditional attitudes and behaviors and to set things straight, she needs and will have to find the support of like-minded women. Old friendships will develop a new focus.

It is important to understand that a woman who aspires to change will be leaving her old circle of friends. Friendships are built on common interests; when these interests change, the friendships change. When you're involved with new ideas and goals, new people who share your aspirations—but probably only a few of your "old" friends—will join you. And don't be surprised if some of your best friends, feeling neglected or threatened by your actions, will "stab you in the back."

Your most effective approach is to look for allies who have similar interests and points of view. The changes you are striving for are difficult enough to bring about even when many people are pulling together, but it's easier if you reinforce and encourage one another.

Women have to stop complaining about the existing power structures and role models. They must stop suffering senselessly, because that won't get them anywhere. They have to be on the alert to keep each other from backsliding into old behavior patterns. They must stand by one another to get over the rough stretches in their struggle.

Change always takes time; it is a long and tedious process, no matter whether it's personal or social change. But changes in social structures, for instance, a new positioning of women, take place on many levels. For that reason, it may take generations to make these changes. Even when people understand what is at stake, the road to an eventual change in attitude is arduous and lined with many setbacks. Yet women have to overcome these hurdles. Who else will fight for them?

Nor will women get anywhere by blaming everything on men, by wasting their strength in tirades of reproach or even hatred of the other gender. Such attacks will either miss the target or boomerang. What is needed are constructive, not destructive, measures. The only way to get anything accomplished is to take action and not wait for an invitation.

At the workplace men defend themselves against competition from women by casting doubt on "female qualifications." But that doesn't necessarily have anything to do with hostility to women. If you give someone the chance to put half of his competitors out of the running, he will do it. The "gender war" is merely used as a cover for shooting off irrelevant and inappropriate arguments. It's time to bring this out into the open.

Imagine that one of your male colleagues is intimidated by your qualifications, and so he is lashing out with chauvinistic drivel. Don't let that stop you. Stay cool and continue to follow your goals.

Women Block One Another

Women are their own worst enemies. It starts with the ideal of thinness that's become an obsession for many women. These standards usually exist only in the female mind; men don't think about it nearly as much. Women create the norm, promote it, and then put the words into men's mouths. A girlfriend's harmless remark, "You seem to have put on a little weight," has more clout than a man's criticism. Apparently in these matters women take the judgment of other women more seriously than that of men. Most men don't care if their wives weigh a pound more or less. Many don't even notice.

And then there's the notion—only partially true—that men always want to be waited on. Actually everybody likes being waited on. But after they've been given some time to get accustomed to it, men are quite able to come to terms with not finding a hot dinner waiting for them when they come home in the evening. Maybe your hungry husband will grumble a little, but if you feel guilty and immediately jump to, that's entirely your own fault. At this point you must say "no." First to yourself, and later to him.

To preclude any misunderstanding, let me repeat:

Men probably prefer to see women as dependent creatures, and they set snares for any woman who wants to be self-reliant and live independently. But the greatest hindrance to women's progress lies within women themselves.

How Can A Woman Recognize Her Own Submissive Behavior?

In this section I will confine myself to individual behavior patterns and the question: How can a woman get a grip on her specific situation? How can she *recognize* her submissive behavior, and how can she change it?

Submissive behavior is often concealed behind "good" feminine traits, which really *are* good when they come from inside a person, when what you do and what you want coincide. But most of the time you act on impulse, without weighing what mid- and long-term effects your own behavior will have. The momentary effect may be positive; perhaps you avoid a fight. But in the long run the losses could be considerable: a lowered feeling of self-worth, or illness, to mention only two possible consequences.

How can a woman know whether she acted from her own conviction, her own interests, or whether she was primarily signaling her readiness to submit?

If you feel bad after you have been helpful, then you've fallen into a trap!

The Compliant Woman

A few examples:

Ellen: He wants to go to an Italian restaurant; she'd rather eat Greek. To avoid a long discussion, she decides it's not that important to her and gives in.

Charlotte: He wants to go on an action-packed outdoors vacation; she'd rather go to a place with culture. She thinks, "Oh, it'll do me good to get some exercise," and gives in. So canoeing on the Salmon River is the order of the day, and just as in previous years, he shoots ahead of her, paddling his canoe with all his might.

Becky: They've already moved five times because of his job; the sixth move is pending. She refuses. After all, she now has an interesting job she doesn't want to give up. But her "Downy-soft" conscience makes her feel guilty, and she melts like butter. Standing in the way of his career would be going too far. She'll just have to look for another job.

Angelica: He wanted children—two, close together. When the second one was on the way, he swore that he'd be a New Man; he'd take paternity leave. End of story? Not quite. She's at home taking care of the kids. Right after the second baby was born, his big chance turned up at work. It was a vice president's job at the head office—in London. He went there by himself, "for the time being."

Women have to figure out what their motivations are:

Ask yourself, When I say or do such and such, is it because I really want to? Or do I behave that way because others expect it of me, or because I assume they expect me to behave that way?

Find out what advantages you get from your present behavior. And ask yourself what advantages you expected to get.

In crucial situations, find specific answers to these questions:

What do I want?
What are my motives?
What do I expect in return for behaving a certain way?
Are there other ways that can get me to my goal?
Are there alternative gestures, different ways of saying things or behaving I could use besides the ones that come immediately to mind?
What is my mood at this very moment?
What would I like to do most?
What is best for me?
What might happen if I go through with this?
What fears keep me from doing it?
How do I feel when I realize that I am ignoring my own interests and thereby denying myself?
How will I feel about this—tomorrow, next week, next month, next year?
In the past, how did I feel in similar situations?

The purpose of this exercise is to uncover your own dependent behavior, which, it's true, is to some extent present in all women. But only after discovering it in yourself can you work out your personal defense strategies.

Submissiveness has many faces. I have divided them into three categories in order to make them easier to identify:

Rituals of submission are actions that signal submissiveness, compliance, and humility.

Gestures of submission are nonverbal ways of expressing submissiveness—body language, facial expressions, gestures.

Language of submission refers to the spoken word, your choice of words, as well as metamessages, that is, the things said "between the lines," and your tone of voice.

Within these three categories you can ferret out messages of submission that lead women to undermine their own development and make it easy for others to take advantage of them. This is unwitting self-sabotage.

Unwitting Self-Sabotage

By her submissive behavior, a woman confirms existing prejudices about male superiority. A woman who behaves meekly or submissively reinforces the imbalance of power and her own low rank in the power structure. She is selling herself short. She accepts barriers that *she* will have great difficulty surmounting later on.

Rituals of Submission: A woman who is the manager of a firm maintains a "polite" front toward an insolent male department head. She reacts with ceremonial courtesy. She uses friendly words, her voice remains calm, subdued. She smiles when he interrupts her. He calls her "my dear woman" and lectures her in a booming voice. But she has no focused defense strategy. At a meeting, she permits him to give her a dressing down in front of all the department heads.

Another woman, who is head of a company's human resources department, pulls the files she needs out of the cabinets herself, delaying important work because she doesn't want to bother her secretary who probably would have to waste a lot of time searching. She is demeaning herself.

Gestures of Submission: Assume that you are repeatedly assigned to do petty tasks. You say, "No," but *at the same time you smile apologetically and shyly lower your eyes.* That's like saying, "Try again, maybe I'll say 'yes' next time because refusing to do it makes me feel lazy, mean, and petty."

Language of Submission: You're sure of yourself and the subject under discussion, so you express your opinion. But you tag retractions onto the ends of your sentences: "That's right, isn't it?" or "Don't you agree?" By doing that, you give the opinions of others more weight than your own.

Short-Term Advantage(s) of Submission

The question is: What are the advantages of submission? Many women bend and buckle and end up thinking that smiling, pleading, crying, whining, and being "good" are appropriate feminine strategies for success. And at first glance the system seems to work; often there are positive effects initially, and usually there is the hoped-for reaction. For example, the nice little girl who gives away one of her candies receives praise. The good, grown-up girl who does overtime and finishes the work others should have done is praised. The helpless-looking woman driver gets assistance in changing her flat tire, and all the things that might frighten a timid wife are cleared out of her way.

Barbara was one of those women who fled professional challenges by becoming submissive. After seventeen semesters, she finally got her college degree. But then for years she couldn't find work and was supported by her husband. Her rationale was clever: She touted herself as an intelligent college graduate who was too good to work as a typist while she was looking for the right job in her own profession. For a while people believed her. But when she finally found her dream job, it didn't last long. She became pregnant. She literally fled from professional responsibility into motherhood. The escape was made easy for her. Pregnancy is an acceptable way for women to dodge professional stress. The price she paid, however, was high. Her spouse made more and more demands at home. He didn't pay much attention to the baby, and she was left to cope with all the domestic problems. So there may have been a short-term advantage, but the injury that her submissive behavior caused was serious and lasting.

It starts deep within: The fabric of your self-worth develops cracks. The hoped-for respect from others isn't forthcoming. This is unavoidable, and your expectation that other people will believe in you more firmly than you believe in yourself is bound to be disappointed. The consequences don't appear until later on when, after continual discontentment, you suffer from exhaustion, fatigue, and even symptoms of illness. The effect all this has on your colleagues, friends, and acquaintances becomes apparent when they gradually lose touch with you.

Building Your Own Prison

Afterward, the causes and connections that led you to this pass are hard to discover. The beginnings usually go years back. Perhaps it all started with a seemingly innocuous adaptive behavior on your part: an annoyance you swallowed with a smile; suppressed anger during a family celebration; your willingness to *understand* a girlfriend's behavior. You probably didn't recognize the first warning signals—little hints like the helpless smile you smiled that reflected your disappointment and resignation, the tension in your neck and shoulders, a rumbling stomach, backaches, and headaches.

When women adapt to prevailing circumstances, they confirm the prejudices that generations of women have been fighting against. They wait for someone to rush to their aid; they hope to be rescued from unpleasant situations. This is learned behavior. The insidious thing about it is that sometimes it works—though only for a short while. Research has shown that boys are urged to solve problems on their own, but girls are given help, and difficulties are moved out of their way. So they think this will continue even after they are grown-up. They're caught in a Catch-22 situation: If they accept a challenge, they'd have to do something on their own initiative, whether it's changing a tire, starting a new job, or organizing a trip. It would mean getting their hands dirty, working hard, and coping with setbacks. In other words, taking responsibility for themselves and for the consequences of their actions. On the other hand, there is the alternative of waiting until someone comes along and offers to help them out of their dilemma. That may be only a short-term fix.

Lois, for instance, thought she couldn't drive a car anymore. It all started quite innocently. Ever since she had started living with her partner, he had almost always done the driving. He drove faster than she, and she didn't want to have to listen to his snide remarks when she was at the wheel. She felt uneasy when he drove fast, but that was still easier to take than his "clever" comments about her driving. It all reached a critical point when she was involved in two fender benders. After that, she drove less and less often, and soon she felt so insecure behind the wheel that she smashed into a wall while backing up. She had proved to herself that she really couldn't drive—even though those two previous accidents were not her fault. Her father had always thought she was a bad driver. Whenever she was about to leave the house, she had to listen to his long litany of "tips" for the road. Now she thinks that he was probably right about her driving.

Lois came to terms with her little handicap. In a way she was even glad that her partner was so lovingly supportive. He did all the major shopping and drove her to her health club or the movies. Her inability to drive seemed to have its benefits. It was a good deal easier to be driven around. And it was nice to know that someone was there when you needed him. So, all in all, an advantage, right?

Well, hardly. Lois is virtually a prisoner. Every step she takes is controlled by others. Her dependency is getting worse, and pretty soon she won't be able to make any decisions by herself. An invisible spiral has been initiated. She is getting more and more fearful and less and less able to cope. Eventually there'll be nothing she can do by herself. She'll always need her partner, yet even when he is with her she often feels a vague and undefinable anxiety.

Lois is not unique. Many women live with powerful everyday fears that shackle them to hearth and home. Almost always these fears have taken possession of them imperceptibly. And often the fear prevents them from making decisions that might induce them to break out of the ruts of their marriage. It sounds bizarre, but fear has an advantage too, at least for the short term.

Early Roots

The course for such a restricted life is often set in childhood when parents, other adults, or older children influence the formation of norms and role expectations. It is during this time that the foundation of one's self-image is laid: whether individuals think of themselves as strong, intelligent, and mathematically inclined, or helpless, weak, and dumb. In the first weeks of their children's lives parents are already unwittingly beginning to educate them as either boys or girls. Bringing up and educating a girl is practically tantamount to teaching her to be helpless. Girls learn early that they can do few things by themselves. A helping hand will remove obstacles before they even recognize them as such.

Unintentionally mothers spend less time nursing baby girls than baby boys, they touch them less, and don't pick them up and hold them in their arms as often.

Even today little boys wear blue outfits, and little girls wear pink. And so later on, the blue work suit is still typical dress for men, whether it's an elegant pinstripe or dirty coveralls.

Mobiles with flowers, dolls, or angels float over a little girl's crib, whereas airplanes, cars, horses, and ships dangle over a little boy's. The boy finds out very early what his future world will be. He's already playing pilot in the nursery. Nobody is surprised that even in their first months, girls show more interest in pictures of people, and boys in pictures of things.

Even though experts may differ on the question of whether certain behaviors are inherent or acquired, the fact remains that gender-specific education begins in infancy, if not in the womb. It's a boy because it kicks so hard—masculinity is attributed to the fetus because it is so active. It's sure to be a strong, capable, and self-confident boy!

In contrast, rambunctious girls are bad girls. They just want to annoy their mothers. Girls are taught to play for the sake of the game, not to win. They're always supposed to be friendly and polite. They are trained for harmonious relationships and educated to be peacemakers.

Little girls aren't supposed to have beastly wills of their own. Every time a little girl wants to have her own way and wants to follow her natural urge to be active, she is considered bad, stubborn, and willful.

Her father looks at her with disdain and anger. He would certainly have excused this behavior in a boy. Boys are "naturally" defiant; they have to have their way now and then. They have to sow their wild oats; it's healthy.

And so happy, lighthearted children are molded into tough guys and sweet ladies.

In elementary school, girls can still get away with boisterous behavior, but later they are relentlessly trained to be ladylike. Mistakes are tolerated only for a short time; in adolescence or earlier, the pressure is intensified. The girl who doesn't bend loses the acceptance and affection of both adults and her peers. The grown-ups warn her that so-called heavenly (wedded) bliss will be denied her; and the little gilded gate on the glittering and desirable cage threatens to snap shut in front of her nose. Then, if all these threats don't work, people suspect that something isn't quite right about her. Today it is more difficult to uncover the subtle way in which gendered behavior is instilled in children. There is a genuine effort nowadays to raise children in a gender-neutral way; consequently gender-specific patterns disappear under a camouflage net of generosity, liberalness, and tolerance. And so the old prejudices are unintentionally confirmed: that women are less aggressive, less interested in technical things, more passive, less independent, and less ambitious than men; that they are creative in activities using fine-motor skills—they do arts and crafts, knit, embroider, make pottery—whenever possible, things for their families to use.

All those traits considered naturally feminine or naturally masculine in later years are subliminally implanted in early childhood, indeed, already in infancy. Later these qualities are interpreted as genetic or inborn.

The earlier behavior is learned, the harder it is to recognize it as acquired. But anything that is *acquired* can also be changed.

When a little girl toddles away from her mother's side, she is immediately picked up, caressed, *and* held tight. She will be pulled back from her little adventure more quickly than a boy of the same age. And so she learns that it is wrong (dangerous? unseemly?) to explore and conquer the world for herself.

The most obvious way little girls are drilled to focus on people, to be interested in human beings (more than in facts and objects), is by giving them dolls as presents while they are still infants. Little girls are already cradling their dolls when they are barely ten months old. Some researchers call this the doll-cradling reflex. Are they being ironic or is this a grave misinterpretation? It is wrong to interpret such behavior as mothering instinct. It is the evidence of a constant drill in femininity.

The list of examples of how little children grow into typical men and typical women is long. Some are obvious and familiar. Everybody knows how a girl is taught to play with dolls, and boys are given more technical toys. But the following cases are also common. A teacher reports enthusiastically how pleased she is when the little boys in her class play tricks on her. She is amused at the clever and impish ways they think up to break the rules and ignore their assignments. With a smile she admits that though sometimes she protests a little, most of the time she quietly tolerates it. There are overtones of admiration in her voice as she describes how—with only mild disapproval—she condones their not keeping their promises. Boys make her feel insecure, but she doesn't let the girls off so easily.

Boys get more toys. Girls, for the most part, get useful presents—right through to their hope chests. Boys have fun; girls prepare themselves for their roles as housewives. Girls are often excused from certain tasks: They don't have to carry heavy things. Are they too weak? During their monthly periods they are not supposed to participate in sports, or swim. Are they sick?

Girls are continually warned, "Be careful! You can't be too cautious; dangers lurk everywhere." They are taught, "for their own good," never to take risks, and so their chances to win later on in life are reduced. They remember the warning "There are risks involved in trying to win." And so competition by women is elimi-nated early in the game.

It is an insidious pitfall for a woman to believe that someone who hurts her really has only her best interests at heart. She thinks that behind the patronizing behavior, the sanction, and the "support," there is a noble, unselfish wish to help, for which she ought to be grateful—even when the consequences aren't to her advantage. "What counts is the other person's good intentions." The woman is in a double bind, namely the two messages contained in the be-havior conflict. She is caught up in a situation that makes her help-less. No matter how she reacts, it will be wrong. For example, her boss refuses to give her a promotion under the pretext of being con-cerned for her health: "You'd overextend yourself in that job; it will take too much out of you. I want to protect you against that." The trap here is that if the woman fights to get promoted, she will be considered ungrateful. If she backs down and moderates her de-mands, she will lose her self-confidence.

Making decisions with confidence becomes difficult when you can't tell anymore what is and what isn't good for you. So there's one fact that often stands out after they have learned their feminine roles: Women always pull the short straw and come off second best. They react illogically, talk too much, and are wily and intu-itive. But what a psychologically healthy, mature adult *should* be is analytical, precise, abstract, and direct—in other words, a typical man. Accordingly, women either have a psychological problem, or they act like men! They are unsuited for responsible assignments and are destined to work under someone else's leadership.

At this point you may be saying to yourself, "But it's all differ-ent today—I'm bringing up my child to be an independent adult, no matter whether it's a boy or a girl." Perhaps. But sad to say, the gender stereotypes of our parents and grandparents continue to be relentlessly inculcated. Through their behavior, habits, or family rit-uals, parents often, unintentionally and unawares, pass along ex-actly those things they really wanted to avoid transmitting.

Astrid, a flight engineer, is pregnant; she is hoping for a boy because she thinks boys are naturally more interested in technical things than girls, and more gifted too.

Sophie is five years old. She hardly ever plays with dolls. For her last birthday she got a remote-control toy car from her open-minded mother who is sure that she is bringing up her daughter in a gender-neutral way; the car and Sophie's train set and little tool-box are evidence enough of that. But the trap snaps shut one day when Sophie boldly tries to climb a tree. At that point her alarmed mother pulls her back down.

Betty wants to raise her daughter to be a strong young woman, but she keeps telling her that even if somebody hits her, she must not hit back. She should defend herself with words only, not with her fists. When the little child throws a fit because she lost in a game, Betty explains to her, "You shouldn't play games to win, but to have fun *together* with your friends."

We always fall back automatically into familiar behavioral and educational patterns. It isn't the new broom that sweeps clean, after all, but the old one. And in spite of all your resolutions, you imperceptibly slide into old, familiar behaviors and attitudes; you feel more secure with them. After all, they have become deeply rooted over many generations. From time to time, after making some comment, every mother has suddenly felt uneasy, thinking, "I sound just like my mother. That's exactly what she would have said!"—words she'd sworn would never cross her lips. She feels virtually the same bewilderment she felt in her childhood when her mother talked to her like that. How could she have said that to her own daughter? She's shocked to recognize the same quirks in herself that used to drive the family crazy about her mother; or worse yet, her own children or spouse complain about this very behavior.

Early "educational successes" contribute toward making girls typically female later in life. This feminine behavior is not inherited. It comes from patient inculcation of friendliness, dependency, and adaptability. Unfortunately, it is not customary for girls to re-

ceive early-childhood training in initiative, independence, and assertiveness.

True, girls are brought up to have a certain kind of independence
and self-confidence, but that has to do more with acquiring self-
sufficiency skills like shopping, cooking, and helping their mothers around the house. This has nothing in common with genuine
independence, self-confidence, and a spirit of adventure. It is only
a well-camouflaged form of training to adapt and prepare them for
their future job: catering to others.

Little girls get the idea that once they leave the house, it is dangerous to go just anywhere. It's no coincidence that many women
are afraid to leave the protection and safety of their homes. The fear
of feeling lost outside, of the various dangers that lie in wait for
them, especially at night or traveling abroad, is implanted early.
They've been told it isn't suitable for young women to hang out in
a bar at night or to plan a backpacking trip through Australia.

These well-intentioned warnings become deeply ingrained. In
the end, they have a more profound effect than reality—which is
obviously different. Before it's thoroughly checked out, a situation
is stamped dangerous. And even positive experiences that demonstrate the reverse to be true don't do anything to change basic convictions.

Instead of encouraging them to give free rein to their impulses,
girls are told it would be better for them to stay where they are.
Under the pretense of love and concern for their well-being, girls
are gently shackled. They learn that it is good to seek protection
and to stay in familiar surroundings with familiar people.

Through similarly subtle methods they are given to understand
that they have no talent for mathematics or managerial tasks—for
jobs that are generally considered promising careers for men. Very
early on, girls are relieved of certain burdens, ostensibly to make
things easier for them. But the result is, they are unable to cope.
When they grow up, men politely hold doors open for them and
help them into their coats. One might think they can't dress them-

selves. Men open car doors for them. The price they pay for that is that they have to sit in the seat next to the driver, who decides the route and the speed. Once again they play the passive role. Husbands provide a living for them; in exchange they have to be good homebodies.

Although many people know about the dire results of early solicitous educational practices, unfortunately that hasn't changed the attitudes of parents. It doesn't do a woman much good to know that her mathematical talents were buried and forgotten in childhood. The brake that stops her is ideological, and her awareness is the first tiny step on the way to releasing the brake. In spite of her conviction that she cannot do math, this woman has to prove to herself that she can and that's difficult.

Instead of looking for their own hidden talents, people tend to reinforce their negative self-assessments, even though these are based on the wobbly foundation of an education full of prejudices.

Amy, a seven-year-old, explained to me, "We're not very smart. I can't do arithmetic and write as well as the other kids in my class." Actually, she did just as well as the others. What she meant by "we" was her family, and she was just putting into words what her mother thought. The mother's viewpoint was "We're just plain country people, we're not too smart. Our kids can't really make good progress at school compared to the town kids."

It's possible that Amy wasn't all that intelligent. But I believe that she was held back more by the family's negative self-assessment and the resulting lower expectations than by any lack of ability. That's completely normal for a child. But if a grown woman accepts attitudes and opinions from her childhood at face value and carries them over into her adult life, or if she adopts the untested norms and rules of others, then she can no longer act responsibly.

There's no denying that people take not only the good things from their childhood into their adult life, but also harmful attitudes and behavior. Adults can avoid being governed for the rest of their lives by this childhood baggage. And once they are adults, women need not stick to the advice they were given when they were little girls. Here are a few examples of the old saws and proverbs that children learn; you know some of them from the chapter "The Great Deception":

Women may choose to work, men have to!
(Women's work is unimportant. Men's work is what counts.)
If you want to be beautiful, you have to suffer.
(Women have to suffer.)
A wedding dress solves all heartaches!
(The most important thing in a girl's life is marriage.)
Girls who whistle and chickens that crow should have their necks wrung!
(Women who stand up for their rights and are independent have to be put down.)
Other messages are expressed more directly:
Smile and always be polite, even when you don't feel like it.
Don't ever take your moods out on others.
You can achieve more with a smile than with a thousand arguments.

Any woman who adheres to these old adages is stuck in the role of the inconspicuous good girl; she stokes her own prejudices and confirms those of others.

Deceptive Advantages of Prejudices

From the perspective of social psychology or psychoanalysis, prejudices have a purpose; they serve to separate and enhance one's own group.

They generate a *them-against-us* mentality. Your group dissociates itself from other groups. Within your group you feel solidarity, familiarity, and security. If you deviate from your group's norms, it's like jumping into unknown waters. Either you drown or you feel invigorated. But it takes courage to give up the safe and the familiar.

In addition, prejudices protect existing power structures. That helps people to orient themselves and offers a certain predictability. But it also means the perpetuation of ingrained hidebound behavior and role clichés. For women it means that as long as their behavior confirms existing preconceived notions about the traditional woman's role, they themselves help to maintain their powerlessness.

On the other hand, prejudices shield you from fear and self-criticism. They stabilize feelings of self-worth, both positive and negative. The positive feelings go as far as conceit, and the negative ones may even include inferiority complexes.

Every form of submissiveness keeps a person in a state of dependency. And the more firmly she believes that she fits and belongs in this submissive role or is irrevocably caught in it, the more fixed her dependency will be.

Whenever women are "good," belittle themselves, or smile for no reason, they strengthen those who denigrate, discriminate against, and weaken them.

And worst of all, they sometimes think that they are not worth much. To feel good, they need confirmation from others. This, too, is submission, which can have many faces. Let's look at some of these more closely.

Forms of Submission

Actually, a smile is quite beautiful. It expresses a happy, contented, comfortable feeling. If you smile at someone, you make contact, you offer acceptance. But smiling turns into a trap when women smile inappropriately, when smiling becomes forced. This kind of pasted-on smile reflects self-abnegation.

Smiling turns into submission when it signals, "I'll adapt, I'll debase myself, I'm a 'good girl.' "

Most of the time women don't realize that with their smiles they are sending out a metamessage that makes them helpless and submissive.

Examples:

She smiles pleadingly even though she is making a demand.

Metamessage: Don't take my demand too seriously.

She smiles questioningly, even though she has come to a definite decision.

Metamessage: Do you think my decision is right?

She smiles defiantly but doesn't dare defend herself.

Metamessage: I give up; I have no choice; I'll keep quiet.

She smiles stupidly and hides her intelligence.

Metamessage: I am stupid; I need you; don't be afraid of me.

She smiles in embarrassment even though she has done good work.

Metamessage: It embarrasses me when I'm successful at doing something. I won't let it go to my head.

She smiles good-naturedly and hides her anger.

Metamessage: I am angry, but I don't have the courage to show it.

She smiles coquettishly; she thinks she can achieve her goal only by being coy.

Metamessage: Excuse my awkwardness and stupidity; I always try to be nice. After all, I'm only a woman.

She smiles if she's been caught thinking about herself for once.

Metamessage: I'll never do it again. Sorry.

She smiles helplessly when she can't go on.

Metamessage: I am completely ineffectual; you're the only one who can help me.

She smiles apologetically even though she was right in getting her own way.

Metamessage: I am sorry that I got what I wanted. I'm prepared to rescind it all and do it your way.

She smiles hesitantly even though she's sure of herself in this matter.

Metamessage: I'm willing to change my mind.

Men follow similar patterns. They also want to appease, to avoid direct confrontation. But in their case there are often different, more self-assured metamessages at work:

I am right and will not discuss it any further.

I am sure of my position. I'm sorry if you can't go along with it.

I am king around here. You can say anything you like, but I'll do what I please.

I am only keeping quiet because I don't want to make a scene. That doesn't mean I agree.

The man's metamessage is: *I don't want a fight, but if you have any doubts, I'll go my own way.*

The woman's metamessages say essentially: *I'm not sure; if you have any doubts, I'll moderate my demands.*

The list of submissive smiles is long. And each smile can contain several metamessages.

Women Make Themselves Dependent

When women use their smiles cleverly and coolly to pull the wool over someone's eyes, smiling can be an effective weapon. But when a woman's smile conceals her anger and is primarily intended to soothe her opponent, then it is submission.

In many social situations women follow the prescription to act politely and be conciliatory. If a situation turns critical or unpleasant, they are busy trying to keep their composure. It would never occur to them to defend themselves, or to attack and retaliate.

In addition to the fear that leaves many women no other recourse than a smiling retreat, they're also afraid that they might become unfeminine and unattractive if they were to defend themselves aggressively and vigorously. And so they throttle their natural impulse to fight back. They make themselves helpless. Aggressive impulses are systematically suppressed. (Many women even claim they don't have such impulses.) I believe that choosing not to resist in this way will lead you inexorably to the point where you are no longer taken seriously by other people. At best, a defenseless person arouses pity when she cannot take care of her own interests; she is not accepted as an equal partner or taken seriously in any other way.

By deciding to renounce their ability to fight back, women turn into moral cowards. Unfortunately, if there are many of these unconscious little decisions, a spiral of dependency will be initiated because a defenseless person needs the protection of others. But dependency doesn't end with that. Anyone who voluntarily limits the scope of her activity, that is, who chooses not to use all her capabilities, will become incompetent and helpless in more and more areas. And in the course of time she will have "proved" to herself that she has no abilities at all. Many women believe, more or less consciously, that self-reliance will reduce a partner's willingness to provide protection to them. They are afraid they will have to pay for their independence with a loss of closeness, familiarity, intimacy, and security. So rather than become self-reliant, they make themselves dependent. But just the opposite is true: People who are independent and self-assured manage to cope quite well. If they need support at some time, it is given gladly. The helper in this case knows that he won't be exploited, that this is just a onetime occurrence. Everyone from time to time gets into a situation in which she or he has to ask for advice or a favor.

I would like to mention the role that clothing plays in this connection, but only in passing. The higher the heels, the less secure your footing. The tighter the skirt, the more restricted your freedom of movement. Although some may believe that a woman can achieve everything she wants teetering on high heels, this "charming helplessness" is still a form of self-limitation.

The spiral of dependency keeps turning. Many women sooner or later will also become economically dependent. And that almost always means losing even more of your sense of self-worth.

The spiral could end in serious psychological problems, caused by constant excessive adaptation and submission, and the continual fear of rejection. Somebody who is trying to do everything right for everyone else is no longer aware of closeness and connection to other people. She is weighed down by fears of loss and can't experience the joys of togetherness.

Equal partnership in a serious relationship or marriage is beyond her reach.

Her dependency on parents, husbands, lovers, and superiors escalates. In the end she really can't take care of herself anymore. She is no longer in a position to make her own decisions, to earn a living, to write out a check, or to file a complaint in court.

Chapter 10

Women's
Self-Abnegation
and Renunciation

.

I get furious when I think of the many ways women waive their rights and renounce their own interests. Someone once said, "Self-denial is a woman's disease." This self-denial is usually accompanied by a smile, though the smile is always forced. But there's another side to all this. When a woman uses a friendly smile consciously as a strategy, it's justifiable. It makes it easier for her to accomplish something; it overcomes resistance, and it can soothe ruffled feelings. But if a woman always smiles a fixed smile no matter what her frame of mind, then that's a sick smile.

It isn't simple to pigeonhole the various categories of smiles: Is the smile spontaneous or is it functional? That is, is there a particular purpose behind it? And if it's functional, is it accompanied by an eagerness to submit and to pacify someone, or does it reflect a firm inner purpose and the resolve to steer or control another person? I call the first one a *submissive smile,* and the second a *power smile.*

A submissive smile almost invariably is accompanied by gestures or rituals of submission.

Among these are the following actions, which always involve renunciation:

⚠

- Renouncing your right to contradict someone
- Renouncing your intelligence—playing dumb
- Renouncing your right to assert yourself (the ability to have things your way)
- Renouncing your own principles
- Renouncing your right to earn your own income, to attain success and recognition
- Renouncing your right to physical space and time of your own

The decisive aspect of submission is the act itself. The smile is simply a signal that an act of submission is about to take place.

Renouncing Your Right to Talk Back

Women seldom answer back; they accept almost every burden that's laid on them, without protest.

Enid described how she constantly had to put up with being interrupted at work. Her desk stands in a room that leads to another. Whenever people come walking through, she feels she has to return their greetings, at least with a smile. Her job involves entering complex columns of numbers into a computer, and every time she looks up to say hello, she loses her place. She's never complained about this to her boss.

Wilma, another "good girl," works full-time as a salesperson in a boutique. She is "happy" when she can do others a favor, even if it means canceling her own plans. She's supposed to work late every fourth Thursday. But in the last six months, she has worked late nineteen Thursdays—without getting overtime pay. No one else had worked that many evenings. The woman with the next highest number had worked only five. Good girls will uncomplainingly give up money they've earned. They're hoping that they'll be liked for their friendliness. Fat chance. This attitude won't get them ahead.

They rub their eyes in amazement when some unfriendly, egotistical "old battle-ax" gets promoted ahead of them without losing the sympathy of the other workers. Gossips say nasty things, but the remarks are also tinged with admiration, and secretly or even openly they look for a nod of recognition from these "power women."

I have limited myself to only a few examples of women in the workplace who don't talk back, because usually this smiling renunciation is easy to identify. These women are indirectly sending the message:

"Nobody will like me for myself."

"If I'm stubborn, no one will want to have anything to do with me."

Renouncing the Use of Your Intelligence—Playing Dumb

Women are often content to define themselves through their looks and their readiness to comply. They think that the more beautiful a woman is, the more desirable she is. And the more compliant she is, the greater the chances that the relationship with her partner will last. For that she is prepared to relinquish all the other qualities that allow a person to become self-confident and independent. She gives up using her mind, she gives up thinking critically or acting purposefully.

She doesn't strive for intellectual fulfillment and only takes on challenging work as a last resort. She certainly would like to have a respectable job and earn decent wages. But that's not absolutely necessary, and she doesn't want to invest a lot of effort in it.

She feels it's enough if she's married to a man who has a good job or prospects for one. Once that's accomplished, she'll look for a part-time job; after all, she does need something to keep busy. This strategy isn't half-bad for the woman who simply must have a husband, at any cost. Studies have found that the more money a woman earns—that is, the more financially independent she is—the harder it is for her to get married.*

---

*Faludi, Susan, *Backlash: The Undeclared War Against American Women*. New York: Anchor Books/Doubleday, 1991.

Other surveys* demonstrate that there is a correlation between intellectual challenge and decreasing concern about one's looks. In so-called shopping surveys, pollsters found that the more satisfied a woman was in her job, the less often she bought clothes.

Little girls learn quite early in life that looks, supposedly, are more important than brains. When they reach puberty, self-assured, daring girls—provided they had the chance to develop these potentials—turn into insecure giggling teenagers who care only about their appearance. They lose their lighthearted spirit. Energetic, boisterous, robust young girls become unprepossessing, delicate, fragile creatures. Now they compete only over who's the prettiest in the class, who does the best job with her makeup, who wears the "in" clothes. Schoolwork isn't important anymore.

At class reunions decades later, the women rarely remember a classmate's skill on the debating team, her get-up-and-go, or her spontaneity in pursuing her own goals. What they do remember is what the other students looked like rather than their talents and abilities.

In addition, many women remember for the rest of their lives the pain they felt because of physical shortcomings. They suffer because their legs are too thin, their breasts too big or too small, their hair is the wrong color or it isn't curly, and their eyes are too close together or too small.

Even today girls still shed tears over the same "tragedies." They spend hours trying to make themselves look like the current beauty idol, and they suffer profoundly if it doesn't work. From the time they're little, they practice how to please.

There are many other tacit renunciations of intellectuality, such as:

"Since I don't have anything else going for me, I at least have to look well groomed."

"A pleasant appearance will get you further than intelligence."

---

*Ibid., p. 246.

Renouncing the Right to Assert Yourself

The inability to assert yourself is just as subtle a form of submission as the previous renunciations. I run across examples of this in my seminars every day. In defending themselves, women speak much too softly. Their opposition, their criticism, and their anger fizzle out ineffectually. If they are exploited or treated unjustly and disrespectfully, they submit silently.

For the last three years Florence had been working half days for the owner of a small firm. She has been doing all the office work. Before his vacation started last winter, her boss asked her to work full-time while he was away. Florence agreed immediately and as a matter of course. But her next paycheck did not include compensation for a single hour of the extra time she had put in. When she asked when she would be paid for the additional time, her boss became indignant. After all, he said, she had done it as a favor to him, and anyway there wasn't much she had to do except take a few telephone calls. Florence could only mumble something under her breath; she was afraid to make her boss angry and to lose her reputation as a dedicated and dependable employee.

Months later, the boss's wife told Florence that her husband didn't have money to throw around, and since there had been no prior agreement, he didn't have to pay her for the additional hours she had worked. But if she had made a scene, the boss's wife said, there's no doubt he would have given her the money. The advice came too late. Florence became more and more dissatisfied with her work and couldn't shake the feeling that she had been cheated. Half a year later she gave notice. She never got the money.

People rarely give you what you've "earned" if you don't ask for it.

Mary is a department manager in a large company. Her assistant often goes over her head, even when it comes to important decisions that he should definitely discuss with her first. Mary is very upset about this, especially since she rarely approves of his decisions. Still, she doesn't put him in his place. Nor does she reverse his decisions, even when they are wrong and could cost the company a lot of money. She doesn't want him to lose face in front of his co-workers, so she pretends that she participated in making the decisions.

You can't handle this sort of disrespect with kind words and patience. There's only one way for Mary to assert herself permanently. She must firmly reprimand her assistant, reverse his bad decisions, inform the other employees of what happened, and define each worker's responsibilities.

Women often "defend" themselves against charges that they are not sufficiently aggressive by offering questionable excuses such as:

"My feminine style of leadership has to be in clear contrast to the aggressive males."

"Once I've reprimanded a male employee, he won't trust me anymore."

It's hard to turn your back on female "virtues."

Renouncing Your Own Principles

For the most part women tend to obey social norms, even when they don't feel good about doing it. They doubt *themselves,* never the rules.

This type of renunciation is especially obvious among many mothers who believe that during the early years of their children's lives they should be at home with them.

However, several studies point out that the baby does quite well without having his mother constantly hovering over him or her.

Even mothers who have doubts about the validity of the old conventions still stick to them, if only indirectly. The excuse they give is that they wouldn't be able to enjoy their children if they were working all day. However, research shows that working mothers and nonworking mothers spend about the same amount of time with their offspring. This refers to quality time spent with the child, reading aloud, playing, etc., *not* carpooling, meal preparation, and that sort of thing.

And yet, every year hundreds of thousands of women submit to the old saw that a good mother's place is with her child. Then, having stopped working for some time, they find returning to the job is considerably more difficult than they were led to believe. In 1995, there were 1.1 million unemployed women twenty years and older reentering the labor force in the U.S. Over thirty-four percent remained unemployed for more than fifteen weeks with twenty percent unemployed for twenty-seven weeks and longer.

One personnel department head put it this way: "The [women] applicants clearly showed they weren't really interested in working." Women had complied with an outmoded rule and now they were being branded as unreliable job candidates in the workplace!

The thinking that imprisons women within these traditional attitudes goes something like this:

"If I do what most other mothers do, I run less risk of doing something wrong in raising the children."

"If I don't stick to the accepted rules, I'll be held responsible if something goes wrong. Nobody will back me up, there'll be nothing but criticism."

In my opinion such attitudes represent a very serious denial of one's own ideas and principles. If women want to break down female role models, then a change of the rules is imperative. That means saying good-bye to housekeeping dos and don'ts. Making the beds every day, dusting once a week, cooking at least one hot meal a day for the family, and a lot of other routines are passé. Not leaving the house without makeup on, being concerned about making a good impression (that includes what the children wear), supervising the kids' homework, and doing all the housework every day—these *can't* be the most important things in a woman's life.

Renouncing Your Right to Financial Independence

When I demand economic independence for women or from women, I encounter heaps of opposition. Women would like to believe in a contract between the sexes guaranteeing that males will provide them with material security. They forgo their own entitlement to pensions, professional challenges, and owning property.

Women make up fifty-two percent of all high school graduates and more than forty-six percent of all college graduates, yet only five percent of all company executives are women. The numbers speak for themselves. By saying "no thanks" to demanding, challenging occupations or professions, women perpetuate their meager share of power in society.

Renouncing Additional Training, College, or Professional Education

Girls and young women are rarely aware of the consequences their decision to do without higher education or professional training may have on their futures. They would rather put themselves in the hands of some man about whom they as yet know nothing, but to whom they involuntarily cede their future opportunities in life.

Della was studying dentistry with the idea of taking over her uncle's practice since he had no children of his own. But she gave up the chance to finish her studies in order to marry a biology student. Both she and her husband have well-to-do parents who subsidized the "student household." After getting his degree, however, her husband couldn't find a decent job, and now barely keeps his head above water as a traveling salesman. Della suffered because of his problems and told me how sorry she is that he couldn't land a good job commensurate with their accustomed lifestyle. She is ashamed of *his* failures. It doesn't occur to her that *she* could be contributing to their livelihood. She thinks the fact that she didn't become a successful dentist makes things easier for her husband. "Otherwise he'd be even more despondent," she says. She certainly could have become a dentist, but the idea that she should now go out and work doesn't enter her head.

Sonja had been working as a clerk in a drugstore. She went to night school to get her high school degree. After that she wanted to study pharmacy. But then she met a man who was not a college graduate. She thought that he'd feel uncomfortable if she had a better education than he did. So she dropped her plans to study and became a housewife and mother.

These are examples of women who had terrific opportunities to get a professional education. Women in less fortunate circumstances give up continuing with their education much more often. For women who drop out of high school, it means getting a job in a factory, supermarket, or a Burger King. They take an entry-level job and are happy that they're earning more than a girlfriend who is going to night school and working part-time.

The plan is the same no matter what their educational level. After getting their basic education, many women give up the chance to get a professional degree.

Renouncing the Right to a Successful Career

The chain of renunciation continues after a woman marries and has her first child. For almost all women, motherhood signifies an outright break in their careers; for many it means a career nosedive.

If a woman's earnings are not essential to the family budget, then as a rule she puts off returning to work for quite a long time. Consequently, her prospects for adequate professional opportunities grow steadily worse.

But some women—even after they get a degree and have excellent prospects—will give up the chance of going into a profession.

Margaret and her husband had both studied forestry. After graduation Margaret did not try to get a job. She would have had to apply for the same openings as her husband, and that sort of competition seemed to her "devious." Actually, she had done better at school than he and would probably have done better in interviews. When I spoke with her, about four years later, she still had not accepted a job. She and her husband moved to one of the western states where he works in a forest preserve.

Women who believe they can safely make it without an income of their own are creating the foundations for their own servitude.

Inadequate education, long employment gaps, not going for advanced training—these are the pieces that make up the mosaic of a dependent life.

I have discussed this problem with dozens of women, and over and over again they confirm that someone who has to ask for permission to spend money will always somehow feel beholden. Such a woman can't possibly develop a feeling of self-esteem, nor is a genuine partnership likely under these circumstances.

The Shrunken, Diminished Woman

Not only are women willing to put up with not having their own incomes and financial independence, but they also renounce having time of their own and a room of their own—the two are often related. Even women with incomes of their own are quite willing to do this. Renunciation is evident in their body language. In an earlier chapter I described how women often make themselves small or thin—and not only to conform to an ideal of beauty.

Nowadays women rarely have a "room of their own." Only a few have such a place in the family's home. Some have a room—usually as big as a pantry—where they sew or iron. And they have that space only because (a) they perform services for the family there, and (b) so that the ironing won't clutter up the other rooms. A woman is supposed to think of the entire apartment or house as hers; that way, she's responsible for keeping it all clean and in order. She's forced to adjust her needs for time of her own to those of the family. If women friends come over for a cup of coffee, they disappear as soon as the husband arrives. She can sit down with a book only until somebody turns on the television. And if she's having a long chat with a friend on the phone, she has to use the phone in the hall.

A woman will arrange her day so that nobody gets shortchanged. But she doesn't consider her own wishes. She takes time out for herself only if there's any time left over. And that almost never happens. Then, even if she's decided some evening or on a weekend to leave part of the housework undone, she's usually too exhausted to do anything enjoyable.

By her behavior the shrunken woman indicates, "What I do isn't important. I don't require a particular place or time for myself. I have no interests of my own that require peace and quiet." Many women follow this principle in their everyday lives. They do without space of their own and are quite ready to move aside. If a man and woman come toward each other on the sidewalk, ordinarily it's the woman who steps aside. Even though the common rule of courtesy grants a lady the right of way, it's usually only the attractive or self-confident women who get it—which makes it so much worse.

⚠

- **Don't avoid confrontation!**
- **Give yourself sufficient room to move around in!**
- **Stand up for your right to be left undisturbed!**

At work, women are often assigned distinctly smaller and poorly situated offices. One executive secretary told me that the "kitchen cabinet," the coffee machine, the sink, and the garbage can were all in her office. Every few minutes someone would come in, say hello, talk to her briefly, make coffee, throw away leftover food, or rinse an apple in the sink. Whenever this happened, her work would be interrupted. Nobody paid any attention to her protests. They said she was hostile, putting on airs and pretending to be doing complicated work that required concentration. She, on the other hand, didn't want to give the impression that she was snooty. Nobody took her seriously, and no wonder. A sidelong look, a lifted eyebrow, were enough to squelch her and keep her from complaining.

But no longer. Today there's a sign on her door: PLEASE DO NOT DISTURB. And even the department heads comply after she finally dared to speak up and let out her anger about her miserable working conditions.

Just as they make do without adequate space, women also make do without time of their own.

Elizabeth was proud that she always had "enough time for every-body." She felt it was a virtue to always have time for others. She would never let anyone wait if she could possibly help it. It didn't matter what it was that was wanted from her or what she was doing at the moment—she simply stopped doing it, even if it was some-thing very important to her personally. Other people always had precedence. But even so, Elizabeth still feels she's not "good" enough—she's often annoyed with her own impatience. She gets fidgety when people stay too long, and immediately feels guilty be-cause she isn't sufficiently "friendly."

Because she feels unimportant, she always submits to the time dictates of others. When her children (ages thirteen and sixteen) want to talk to her, she stops reading and turns her attention to them. When the grandparents want to come for coffee on Sundays, she calls off the walk she was planning to take with friends and spends the time with Grandma and Grandpa.

In the evening, when friends stay very late, she smiles and hides her yawns so that her guests will not feel she's chasing them out.

For powerless people, having time for others is a "privilege." But powerful people are stingy with their time. They claim they have "no time," meaning that they have more important things to do.

On the other hand, the poor, the unemployed, the powerless, and women always have time. They have time to give away.

"Time is money" applies only to those who concentrate on their work and hang a DO NOT DISTURB sign on their office doors.

Powerful people's time is an expensive commodity. To get to see them, you have to make an appointment. And not everybody will be granted time. The more powerful the individual, the fewer peo-ple will be given access to him. A female boss doesn't enforce this rule. She thinks her door always has to be open. It's the new, fem-inine style of leadership: the open door, a symbol of empathy and sensitive leadership. She always has time for everybody. This is an-other way of submission.

Like all other underprivileged people, women cannot dispose of their time as they please. A wife adapts to her husband's time requirements. On warm summer days, hordes of women stream out of swimming pools between four o'clock and four-thirty so that they can be home ahead of their husbands, prepare their suppers, greet them at the door.

Only last week I witnessed an ugly scene. A husband, coming home from work, shouted at his nearly grown daughter, asking where her mother was. Didn't her mother know that this was the time he always came home and wanted his drink before dinner? Usually the mother is there and ready every evening, but this time she had been delayed. His enraged bellow echoed through the house. Was someone perhaps rattling the power structure? This had to be stopped before it got out of hand!

This scene is not exceptional. Every evening, every Sunday, every vacation, and every holiday, women and children jump to the husbands' and fathers' timetable. Some of them manage to sneak away under some pretense or other, but many function quite well. After all, he's the one who brings home the bacon. Whoever has the money has the power. That may be a truism, but it's also a reality.

Also, whoever has power can not only control his own time but also other people's time—in private life as well as on the job.

A wife's status is lower than her husband's; she has no more right to keep him waiting than an employee would keep his boss waiting, or a patient his doctor. If a wife doesn't wait for her husband, he's going to assume that he is losing status in the family. Apparently, he'll think, she has more important things to do. It's a threat, and so he aggressively defends his domain.

Many of you know what it's like waiting for an examination or a job interview to get under way. The longer you have to wait, the more restless you get, and the more your feeling of self-worth sinks. If the waiting time exceeds your tolerance threshold, you find yourself getting desperate. By then, you can no longer adequately present yourself and your abilities.

The proposition that a woman always has time is unfortunately confirmed by the behavior of many "good" women. They give up their independence, the right to have time and interests of their own. They end up harried and overworked. Women have allowed others to appropriate their time. They do what they are told. And so they feel pushed around, worthless, incompetent, and stupid.

But "bad" girls are different. Every day they take a certain amount of time in which they do something they enjoy, something that's important to them or that makes them happy. It doesn't matter whether they have a job or are "only housewives." Nor does it matter whether they play tennis, go for a walk, lie down, read a book or magazine, enjoy a leisurely bath, or just twiddle their thumbs and stare into space—they are doing what is good for them, without guilt feelings.

Chapter 11

Bad Girls Get to Go Everywhere
—Even to Heaven . . . on Earth!

.

The rebellious girl isn't a new phenomenon exclusive to our times.

In a way, Florence Nightingale, who founded the first nursing school, was a rebel. She disobeyed her parents, turned down a "promising" marriage offer, and undertook a fierce and prolonged campaign to gain recognition for the nursing profession. Although she was sorry that this caused her mother pain, she nevertheless went her own way: If one is born with wings, one should do everything one can to use them to fly.

Many courageous, aggressive, gutsy women have come along since then, for instance, Golda Meir, surely one of the century's most important women politicians. "Nothing in life happens," she said. "It isn't enough to believe in something. You also have to have the stamina to meet obstacles and overcome them."* Her goal was to win, not just to jockey for position. When she was offered the post of Israel's deputy prime minister, she replied with the now famous words: "I'd rather be a full-time grandmother than a part-time prime minister."

Female economic independence also has a tradition. Coco

---

*Martin, Ralph G., *Golda. Golda Meir: The Romantic Years,* Scribner's, 1988, p. 33.

Chanel knew the value of money, but she gave it a new meaning for women: Money never meant much to me, but the independence I could get with it did. And Chanel had another bad-girl virtue. She demanded that women persevere through conflicts as well as failures: You don't learn from your successes, but from the fiascoes. Her rallying cry was, Put your failures behind you and get on with the job at hand.

These are some of the brightest stars in the constellation of outstanding women. But these days even an ordinary woman, the "next-door neighbor," is showing more spirit and a will to win. The proportion of women choosing independence and starting their own businesses is on the rise. The percentage of working women is growing, the number of mothers who return to professional life relatively soon after having a baby is climbing, and last but not least, more women than men are suing for divorce.

What these women have in common:

They break the rules and make their own.
They make firm demands.
They say NO frankly and clearly.
They don't let anyone make them feel insecure.
They have a vision of the path they want to take.
They think big, not petty, thoughts.
They see to it that they have successful experiences.
They don't want to please at any price.
They are not afraid of criticism.
They don't allow others to squelch them.
They accept the fact that there can be no gain without taking
    risks.
They use their energy to accomplish their own goals.
They are proud of their successes.
They enjoy competition.
They speak frankly and worry less about what others might
    be doing or thinking.

Bad girls want to win.

What it really comes down to is that women are frequently willing to renounce the desire to win.

Women must set their minds to winning. They must want to grow by coping with handicaps and hone their skills by overcoming obstacles. Their chances are good, for perseverance and tenacity are feminine virtues.

Contentious, irritating women get further in life. That's a fact, even though our culture has it that anger, rage, and self-assertion are negative qualities. Moreover, women have been denying their powerful feelings for so long that they have lost touch with them. And so "good girls" often feel a pervasive malaise and easily get sick. Bad girls, on the other hand, have learned to fight purposefully. They accept the idea that you can't have relationships between human beings without some aggressive feelings.

Bad girls are not afraid of aggression—not their own or that of others.

Bad girls use their aggressive feelings of anger as a source of energy—even when they are angry at themselves. *Their* solutions aren't self-doubt and self-destruction, but inner and outer courage.

Anger and rage prompt them to act.

A bad girl is observant and will be able to discover and identify hidden aggression for what it is. She won't knuckle under to people who are trying to use their illnesses to bully her; she's not vulnerable to blackmail. Neither her father's "weak heart" nor her spouse's migraine headaches will keep her from expressing an opinion or making a demand. Within limits she'll be understanding and considerate, but then she firmly goes her own way. She doesn't want to save others, nor does she see it as her life's work to try to find that "tender heart" proverbially hidden under a man's hard exterior. She insists on getting recognition and respect.

She defends herself against "sufferers and malingerers" who are subtly trying to promote their own interests. And she won't let them persuade her that she is making their illness worse by fending them off. She is not afraid to have people think she's heartless.

She knows how to defend herself, even against those who want to "help" her. She knows that under the cloak of helpfulness often lurks a secret aggressor who will block her steps toward self-reliance.

She isn't taken in by the tears or the sensitive and delicate nature or weakness of those who make themselves helpless. She unmasks the helpless, revealing the strength that comes to light as soon as they are forced to fight openly for their status.

A bad girl knows that forgetfulness, supposed misunderstandings, and stalling are forms of indirect aggression that are intended to trip her up. She will defend herself, instead of showing helpless understanding.

This goes for her career as well as for partnership and marriage. She won't let others drive her crazy. Her yardsticks are her own convictions and emotions. If she feels vaguely uneasy, she will look for the reason. In the process, she does not doubt herself but looks for external factors that might be responsible. She doesn't let people who seem to be superficially nice pester her. She doesn't let people who claim they know what's good for her talk her out of facing her troubles, pains, or fears. And she doesn't succumb in panic to people who try to intimidate her the moment she shows the first signs of independence. If someone warns her of disaster when she announces her plans, she is ready to live with the consequences rather than back down.

If she has to choose, she will walk away from other people, but she will remain true to herself.